The Women's Press Ltd
34 Great Sutton Street, London EC1V 0DX

Fadhma Aïth Mansour Amrouche was born in 1882 in a remote mountain village in Eastern Algeria and died in France in 1967. The illegitimate daughter of a young widow, she was sent to a Catholic mission, to save her from persecution and possibly death at the hands of the local community. She was subsequently among the first Berber girls to attend the lay school set up by the French. At sixteen, she married a young Berber schoolteacher and bore eight chidren. An untaught poet and singer of the folksongs of her native Kabylia, she handed on her gifts to her only daughter, Taos, and her son Jean, at whose request she wrote the story of her life in one month in 1946, adding an epilogue after the death of her husband in 1962.

Dorothy Blair was born in Birmingham and has had a long career as a University lecturer in French. Since the 1950s she has specialised in African literature written in French, recently turning her attention more particularly to women writers from the Maghreb as well as Africa south of the Sahara. Her publications include *African Literature in French: A history of creative writing from West and Equatorial Africa* (Cambridge University Press, 1976), *Senegalese Literature: A Critical History* (Twayne Publishers, Boston, Mass, 1984) and translations of numerous works in French by African authors, mainly for the Longman African Classics Series.

FADHMA A.M. AMROUCHE

My Life Story

The Autobiography of a Berber Woman

Translated with an Introduction
by Dorothy S. Blair

The Women's Press

First published in Great Britain by The Women's Press Limited 1988
A member of the Namara Group
34 Great Sutton Street, London EC1V 0DX

First published by Librairie François Maspero, Paris, 1968

British Library Cataloguing in Publication Data

Amrouche, Fadhma A.M.   b.1882
  My life story.
  1. Algeria. Social life, 1882-1967.
  Personal observations
  I. Title
  965'.04'0924

ISBN 0-7043-4093-3

Typeset by Boldface Typesetters, Clerkenwell Road, London EC1
Printed and bound in Great Britain by Cox & Wyman Ltd, Reading

Contents

Introduction

In the following pages you will find a very simple story, simply told. A girl is born in a remote Algerian village in the last quarter of the last century; she marries at sixteen, bears eight children, has two miscarriages, loses one child in infancy, outlives all but two of the others, dies at the age of eighty-five: the story of a woman's life. She did no great things, achieved no greatness, did not mingle with the great (although she did meet one famous French novelist, Jean Giono). But she was a remarkable woman. And it was a remarkable thing that she ever came to write the story of her life.

Fadhma Aïth Mansour Amrouche was born in 1882 or 1883* in the austere, mountainous region of Eastern Algeria known as Kabylia. The Kabyles are Berbers, speaking their own language, Kabyle, and maintaining a close unity, separate from the Arabs, even in exile. Kabylia, like the rest of Algeria, was administered by the French colonial authorities. But the proud, fierce Kabyles retained their own customs, which were as harsh as their climate. The villagers grew subsistence crops of olives, figs, grapes, prickly pears, corn and barley; the richer ones sold their surplus fruit, grain and oil on the local markets; the poorer families were so poor that acorns formed their basic sustenance. Vendettas involving curses and violent deaths were common.

Fadhma's mother, Aïni Aïth Mansour, was a beautiful young woman, a widow at the age of twenty-two with two sons aged six and three, when she became pregnant. In Fadhma's words, 'She was young and foolish. In her own courtyard there lived a young man

* The footnote on p. 25 of the French edition, added by Jacqueline Arnaud, gives the date of her birth as 1882, but Fadhma herself writes that she was sixteen when she married Belkacem-ou-Amrouche in August 1899 (D.S.B.).

from her late husband's family. She fell in love. The inevitable happened.' According to Kabyle tribal custom, which the French had not succeeded in wiping out, short shrift was given to a woman bearing a child out of wedlock: the pregnant woman should have been taken out by her own family into the fields at night, killed and secretly buried, to avoid the shame she would bring on them. But Aïni Aïth Mansour had the wit to seek the protection of the local French Administrator, who put an injunction on her brothers and so saved her life and that of her unborn child. But the village considered the illegitimate toddler accursed, and she was exposed to all the cruelty that an implacable, closed society could inflict. Unable to protect her daughter from injury and possible death, Aïni Mansour resolved to leave her in the care of the nuns in a neighbouring village, but took her away after a year because the child had been whipped till she bled, for some trifling misdemeanor. Before long, the young mother heard that the French colonial administration had opened a school for girls near the garrison town of Fort-National, with boarding facilities. With leaden heart, she parted from her daughter, who was little more than an infant, and who spent the next ten years at the school in Taddert-ou-Fella, under the tutelage of a fine French woman, Mme Malaval, passionately dedicated to the cause of female education in Algeria.

Fadhma Aïth Mansour was thus one of the first girls from Kabylia to attend school. But the very fact of the existence of this school caused a scandal among orthodox Muslims and, eventually, a new Administrator found himself under local pressure to close the school at Taddert-ou-Fella. His parting, cynical words were, 'They're pretty, they'll get married,' ignoring the Kabyle prejudice against educated women.

Fadhma was bitterly resentful of the French authorities, who had sacrificed Mme Malaval to a political cabal and had opened a door for herself only to slam it in her face. She tried unsuccessfully to adapt to the life of a village woman in her mother's home. But her mind was too alert, her sensitivities too acute, she was cut off from books, which had offered her a path to freedom and communication with a wider world. She then found a place working in a Catholic mission hospital near the town of Michelet. Within a year, a young man from a different region of Kabylia, who taught at the school attached to the same mission, picked her out during a service in the monastery chapel. Instinctively, one outsider had found another. Belkacem-ou-Amrouche was the only male offspring of a large, wealthy, polygamous family when his grandfather, the despotic but wise Hacène-ou-Amrouche, removed him at the age of four or five from the influence of his profligate father, Ahmed-ou-Amrouche, and entrusted him to the White Fathers, by whom he was baptised, educated and subsequently employed as a pupil teacher. Belkacem remained an extremely devout Catholic all his life and a protégé of the Fathers. When Hacène-ou-Amrouche was on his deathbed and his grandson asked him what he had done for him (meaning what legacy he might expect), the patriarch replied, 'I have done more for you than for any of the others, I gave you an education. The pen that I put in your hands is worth more than all earthly possessions.' His earthly possessions were indeed to be squandered by his prodigal son, Ahmed.

When the young teacher, whom Fadhma had never met, asked the Fathers to request her hand in marriage, she took the Superior's assurance that 'he is very nice' and agreed. So, at sixteen, she was baptised and simultaneously married Belkacem-ou-Amrouche, who was to be the father of her eight children and her companion for sixty years. She now became a member of the Amrouche clan, whose patriarch, Hacène-ou-Amrouche, had fought at Sebastopol, in the Crimean War, calling it 'the City of Bronze'.

In 1946, when she was already in her mid-sixties, one of her sons, the poet Jean Amrouche, begged her to write down everything she could remember of her life, without selecting what she might consider the most significant events or important facts. So, in the course of only one month, she poured out the following pages, reliving in amazing detail every one of the preceding sixty years, with only minor confusions over dates. They tell of all the pains and hardships of a woman's daily existence: births and deaths, sickness, cold, hunger, poverty, exile, solitude among hard hearts and cruel customs; the jealousies of co-wives in a polygamous society; superstitions in a place where life was cheap and medical attention unknown, except for the occasional presence of the French missionaries, whose hospital seems to have been a breeding-ground for infection and a seedbed for conversion. Epidemic and endemic diseases ravaged the population: smallpox, blindness, a host of undiagnosed, fatal illnesses, but mainly the scourge of tuberculosis, which decimated the original Amrouche clan and eventually, in 1940, took two of Fadhma's own sons. She does not omit what she wore, how she cooked, what they ate, how she clothed her children; the problems of shopping and fetching water in an Arab quarter where she, as a Christian, did not wear a veil, but could not venture out of doors bare-headed; the never-ending searches for a new home for the ever-growing family, and how they managed to transport their few possessions; the lack of privacy and the demands made on the wife, always at the mercy of the extended family.

With a mercilessly observant eye and memory for detail of appearance and character, Fadhma paints portraits of this vast, polygamous family, with all its deficiencies and intrigues. She shows little indulgence to any who fall short of her own high standards, particularly her husband's parents, Ahmed-ou-Amrouche and his senior wife, Djohra. But she is discreetly reserved with regard to her husband, Belkacem. With the Berber woman's respect for the head of the family, whom she calls *Amrar* (the Berber term for venerable elder), she never describes him and never criticises him. We sense that she was the dominant partner, often pushing the more reticent, gentler Belkacem into acting on her decisions, particularly in the major crises in their life. And at his death in 1959 she states how she had always lived under his guardianship and protection but 'he always saw everything through my eyes'. For more insight into the father's role in the family and his character, we must go to Marguerite Taos' fictional account of their life in Tunis, *Rue des Tambourins*.

Between the lines of her story, we can make out Fadhma's own character: courageous, proud, fiercely independent, reserved but quick to take offence; fighting an unremitting battle for her own human dignity; intolerant of wasters and spongers among her in-laws, but generous to those in true need; practical, energetic, relentlessly hard-working and, like her mother before her, 'thrifty as an ant'. Passionately protective of her children, at a time of phenomenally high infant child mortality she fiercely willed them to live and gave them tireless care through their many illnesses; yet she was no blindly indulgent mother – she was strict in their upbringing and tried, mainly unsuccessfully, to correct their faults and discipline their weaknesses, while they grew up to be a constant source of anxiety and disappointment. Hand in hand with her love of nature went her sense of the divine and the spiritual dimension of human existence. While a sincere believer, she was never as devout as Belkacem and she roundly condemned every shade of bigotry, religiosity and intolerance in those who could not accept the good in all and who insisted that one religion was 'better' than another.

In the background to Fadhma's account of her personal life and tribulations lies the shadow of world events: in particular, two world wars (even the echo of the Crimea), revolts in Algeria against the French colonists and, eventually, the Algerian War of Independence which broke out in 1954. In 1914 Belkacem-ou-Amrouche was called up for service in the French army (the whole family was naturalised in 1913) but was rejected for active service as the father of a large family. However, Fadhma knew the anguish of the first child leaving home when her eldest son, Paul, enlisted. It was then that she returned to the consolation of the songs and poems of her native Kabylia. In 1940 Paul committed suicide, although his mother was given to understand that he had died in the Exodus from Paris; only Jean, Taos and Paul's son, Marcel, knew the truth about his end. (I am indebted to Mme Laurence Bourdil, Fadhma Amrouche's grand-daughter, for this information.) 1940 also saw the deaths of Louis and Noël from tuberculosis. When Fadhma and her husband were living in retirement in Kabylia, the Algerian war exposed them to new hardships and dangers – they were caught between the resistance fighters and the French army, to whom they were 'Wogs' like the rest – and precipitated Belkacem's death in 1959.

The leitmotifs of Fadhma Aïth Mansour Amrouche's story are poverty, hardship, maternal devotion, exile, the consolation of nature and acceptance of the will of God. *Mektoub* (God's will be done)! The dominant theme, the pattern of her whole life, is that of the outsider, the stranger: first the illegitimate child, rejected by her mother's family and victimised by the villagers; then the intelligent girl with schooling in a primitive rural society; later, at the hospital, among nuns with bigoted, closed minds, and illiterate companions who did not speak French or share her thirst for reading and natural beauty. In the Amrouche family, she was vilified as the renegade who had stolen the favourite son (his conversion was condoned, but her Christian obligations flouted), the Christian among Muslims, the Kabyle among Arabs, Italians, Sicilians. As she writes, towards the end of her story,

> I have omitted to say that I have always remained 'the Kabyle woman'; never, in spite of the forty years I have spent in Tunisia, in spite of my basically French education, never have I been able to become a close friend of any French people, nor of Arabs. I remain for ever the eternal exile, the woman who has never felt at home anywhere.

Fadhma Amrouche had an instinctive musical understanding and an intrinsic poetic sense although, in writing the story of her life, she made no attempt to create 'literature'. She wrote as she might have spoken, as the memories returned, sometimes with repetitions or lack of transitional details, in the simplest, most spontaneous Fernch style, to which I have tried to be faithful in the English version, even respecting her punctuation. She does not talk much of her musical gifts, and not at all of her poetry, and we must look to others, particularly her son Jean, for testimony to these. She was the repository of a vast store of traditional Kabyle songs, legends, poems, proverbs, which she handed on to Jean and to her daughter Marie-Louise-Taos, both of whom inherited her gift for poetry. Jean Amrouche was well known in his day as a poet, singer and broadcaster with French radio; Marie-Louise-Taos adopted her mother's Christian name of Marguerite and published novels and poems either as Taos Amrouche or Marguerite Taos. She inherited a magnificent natural singing voice from both her parents and although she could not read a note of music and had no musical tuition, she sang instinctively, faithful to the tradition of her mother. She gave many recitals of Kabyle songs throughout Europe and North Africa and some of these were recorded on disc and cassette before she died in 1976. She left one daughter, Laurence Bourdil, an actress, who has supplied me with some of the details of the Amrouche family.

Jean Amrouche also sang the songs of his native Kabylia, always acknowledging that he owed them to his mother:

Snatched from her native land from which she had been exiled for forty years, not a day passed but my mother would launch on the wings of song, in her solitude, messages to the dead and the living, just as her own mother had done long ago, and it was from her that she had learnt most of her songs. She came from a family of *clair-chantants*, and she sometimes speaks of her mother and brothers, to whom the whole village would listen in silence when their songs spread through the streets. She collected songs from the Zouaoua region where she was born, but also from the Aïth-Abbas, my father's region . . .

So Jean and Taos, after Fadhma, sang the songs of exile. In his introduction to *Histoire de ma vie*, Kateb Yacine calls Fadhma Aïth Mansour Amrouche 'the mountain stream that fed the well of spring waters from which the poet Jean Amrouche and his sister Taos drew, from earliest childhood, the gift of poetry that was theirs throughout their lives'. Let Jean give evidence again:

I cannot describe the power her voice has to move one, its incantatory strength. She is not aware of this herself and these songs (Berber songs from Kabylia) are not for her works of art, but the spiritual instruments she uses, like a loom for weaving wool, or a mortar, a flour mill or a cradle. It is a toneless voice, almost devoid of timbre, infinitely fragile and on the verge of breaking. It is rather tremulous and every day inclining more to silence, its quavering accentuated with the passing years . . . With her everything is subdued and interiorised. She scarcely sings for herself; she sings in the first place to deaden or recall a sorrow that is all the sweeter for being without remedy, intimately linked to the sips of death that she takes with each breath she draws. You will say that this is the voice of my mother, and so it is natural that I should be obsessed with it and that it should awaken for me the slumbering echoes of my childhood, or those interminable weeks when we lived with the daily impact of absence, exile or death. That is true. But there is something else: on the ranging octaves of that achromatic voice there floats an infinitely distant nostalgia, a nocturnal light from the hereafter, which brings the feeling of a presence, at once close and illusive, the presence of an interior landscape whose beauty is only revealed insofar as one knows it to be lost . . .

At the time when Fadhma wrote the main part of her life story, during that one month of August 1946, she was living in Maxula-Radès, just outside Tunis, with her husband, Belkacem. Four of her eight children were still alive: Henri, Jean, Marie-Louise-Taos and René. The story was entrusted to Jean, with the understanding that, being written only for her own family to better understand their origins, it was not to be divulged and there was no question of any part of it being published, at least during Belkacem's lifetime, as he had been antagonistic to the project of writing anything. When he died in January 1955 and Fadhma left her home to become an exile once more, living in France alternately with Jean and Marie-Louise, she was at first too shattered to take up her tale. Jean died in 1962, and Marie-Louise prevailed upon her mother to write the short epilogue covering the last sixteen years of her life to date. When she died in Brittany in 1967, her daughter Marie-Louise-Taos took on the task entrusted to Jean of deciding what to do with the manuscript notebooks, and arranged for them to be published in their entirety.

To help the reader find a way through the ramifications of the many family connections and follow the author in her peregrinations, I have drawn up a list of the names and places that occur in her story, with an outline map of Algeria and Tunisia and a chronology of the main dates and events.

The footnotes, unless attributed to the translator or to Marguerite Taos Amrouche, are those provided by Jacqueline Arnaud, who helped to establish the original text published by Maspero in 1968. For greater fluency of reading, I have incorporated Jacqueline Arnaud's explanations into the English text where possible. Unfortunately she died in January 1987, so that I was unable to ask her permission for this, but I must hereby acknowledge her collaboration with Marie-Louise-Taos in editing and preparing the original text for publication.

Dorothy S. Blair

Principal Characters

The more important characters appear in bold type.

Fadhma Aïth Mansour's maternal family

Aïni Aïth Mansour, her mother
Kaci Aïth-Lârbi-ou-Saïd, her mother's brother (the wicked uncle)
Mohand and Lâmara, her half-brothers

The Amrouche clan

Hacène-ou-Amrouche, the patriarch, Belkacem's grandfather
Mohand-ou-Amrouche, Takar-ou-Amrouche, Lloussine-ou-
    Amrouche, Chérif-ou-Amrouche, Hacène's four brothers
Taïdhelt, Hacène's senior wife, head of the Ighil-Ali household,
    Belkacem's paternal grandmother
Ouardia (the Rose), Hacène's youngest wife
Tassâdet, Hacène's daughter by an unnamed wife (he had about
    twenty altogether, at different times), who kept house for him in
    Aïth-Abbas
Aïcha (died of TB) and Fatima, Hacène's daughters by Taïdhelt
Ahmed-ou-Amrouche, Hacène's son by Taïdhelt, Belkacem's
    father
Lârbi-ou-Herrouche, Hacène's son-in-law (Fatima's husband),
    drowned in 1900
Chérif, Madani, Saïd, the three sons of Mohand-ou-Amrouche, and
    Belkacem's cousins

Ahmed-ou-Amrouche's wives:

1. **Djohra**, Belkacem's mother
2. **Megdouda**, known as Douda
3. **Zahra**, the eventual favourite
4. Taljilith, known also as Smina

Ahmed-ou-Amrouche's children:

1. By Djohra: **Belkacem-ou-Amrouche** (Fadhma's husband) born *c.* 1881
                Ouahchia (died of TB 1900)
                Reskia (died of TB 1914)
                Hemama
                Tchabha
                Zehoua
2. By Douda: three daughters
                a son, Mohand-Arab, also known as Abbas
3. By Smina,   a son Ali (died in infancy)

Belkacem's maternal connections

Lârbi-ou-Merzouk (a distant cousin of the Amrouches), father of Djohra, Belkacem's maternal grandfather

Aïni, married to Lârbi-ou-Merzouk, Belkacem's maternal grandmother, who brought him up

Khaled-ou-Merzouk (the accursed) and **Hemma-ou-Merzouk** (the caravan-drover), Aïni's sons, Belkacem's uncles

Djohra, Aïni's daughter, Belkacem's mother

Children of Belkacem and Fadhma

Paul-Mohand-Saïd, born 29 May 1900; died 16 June 1940
Henri-Achour, born 8 September 1903; died December 1958
Jean-El-Mouhouv, born 7 February 1906; died 16 April 1962

Louis-Marie, born December 1908; died October 1909
Louis-Mohand-Seghir, born August 1910; died 20 August 1939
Marie-Louise-Taos, born 4 March 1913; died 2 April 1976
Noël-Saâdi, born 20 December 1916; died 10 July 1940
René-Malick, born 15 March 1922

Principal Place Names

Kabylia, the mountainous region of Eastern Algeria, bordering on Tunis, inhabited by the Berber race of Kabyles.

In *La Grande Kabylie* (Greater Kabylia), Fadhma's home region

Aïth-Manegueleth, the village where the Saint Eugénie Mission Hospital was situated, where Fadhma worked from March 1898 to July 1900

Fort-National, important garrison town near which the school and orphanage of Taddert-ou-Fella were situated

Michelet, nearest important town to Aïth-Manegueleth and the hospital (about twelve miles distant)

Ouadhias, the convent run by the White Sisters to which Fadhma was taken by her mother when she was aged three or four.

Taddert-ou-Fella, the village with the school (founded in 1882 by the French Administrator) that Fadhma attended from 1887 to 1897

Tagmount, the mission founded by the White Sisters in 1894, not far from Fadhma's home.

Taourirth-Moussa-ou-Amar, birthplace of Fadhma's mother and home of her maternal relatives.

Tizi-Hibel, Fadhma's birthplace and the village where her mother lived

Tizi-Ouzou, nearest town and railway station to Tizi-Hibel

In *La Petite Kabylie* (Little Kabylia), home region of the Amrouche family

Aïth-Abbas, the area from which the Amrouche clan originated

Ighil-Ali, the village where the ancestral home of the Amrouche family was situated, with a mission run by the White Fathers, a school and a Christian 'village' for their converts

Tizi-Aïdhel, the home of Hacène-ou-Amrouche, 'the Patriarch', and of the 'upland Amrouches'

In Tunis

Bab-Aléoua, the Arab Quarter where Fadhma and her family lived from 1916 to 1918

Maxula-Radès, about 6 miles south of Tunis, where they bought their second house and lived from 1925 to 1957

rue de la Rivière, the street in Tunis where they bought their first house and lived from 1918 to 1925.

Chronology

1910   August, birth of fifth child, Louis-Mohand-Seghir

1911   January, Belkacem's mother, Lla Djohra, comes to live with them in Tunis, having been repudiated by her husband, Ahmed-ou-Amrouche

1913   Belkacem's whole family obtain French naturalisation
        March, birth of daughter, Marie-Louise-Taos

1914   Outbreak of First World War. Death of Belkacem's sister Reskia from TB

1915   Death of Fadhma's mother

1916   December, birth of sixth son, Noël-Saâdi. Ahmed-ou-Amrouche, Belkacem's father, comes to live with them in Tunis

1918   'The first departure': Paul enlists. Move to the rue de la Rivière. End of war

1921   Henri leaves home

1922   Paul marries Charlotte. Birth of Fadhma's last child, René-Malik

1923   Birth of Paul's son, Marcel. Paul leaves his wife and child and departs for Paris. Ahmed returns to Kabylia to his wife, Zahra

1924   Djohra returns to Kabylia for good

1925   The family moves to Maxula-Radès. Jean leaves for France

1928   Louis leaves for Paris, to live with Paul

1931   'The year of the typhoid'

1935   Belkacem retires from the Tunisian Railway Company

1939   Outbreak of the Second World War. Death of Louis from TB

1940   German Occupation of France. Paul commits suicide. Death of Noël from TB

1941   Marie-Louise-Taos marries artist, André Bourdil

1942   Birth of Marie-Louise's daughter, Laurence

1946   Fadhma writes the story of her life in August

1953   They sell the house in Maxula-Radès and return to Ighil-Ali

1954   Death of Ahmed-ou-Amrouche. Start of the Algerian War of Independence

1956   Evacuation of Christian families from Ighil-Ali; Fadhma and Belkacem take refuge with Jean and Marie-Louise in France

1957   They return to Ighil-Ali

1959   3 January, death of Belkacem-ou-Amrouche. 6 February
       Fadhma closes up her Ighil-Ali house for good and leaves for
       France, living in turn with Jean and Marie-Louise
1962   Death of Jean Amrouche in April. In June Fadhma composes
       the Epilogue to her autobiography
1967   9 July, death of Fadhma Aïth Mansour Amrouche, in
       Brittany
1976   Death of Marguerite Taos Bourdil (Marie-Louise-Taos
       Amrouche)

MAP OF N.E. ALGERIA AND TUNISIA

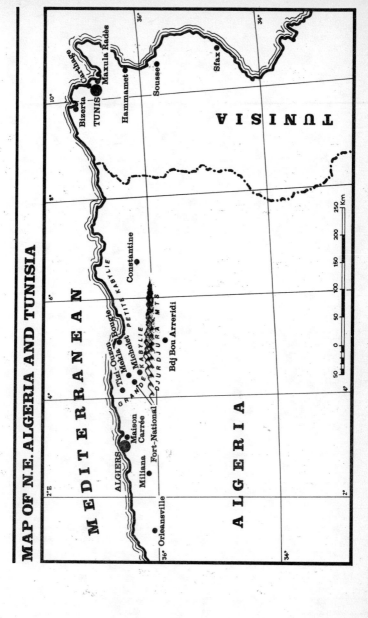

I

The Road to School

My Mother

My mother came from Taourirth-Moussa-ou-Amar, a few miles from Tizi-Hibel, my own village. She belonged to a very good family called Aïth Lârbi-ou-Saïd. She was given in marriage when very young to a man much older than herself, quite an old man who had a daughter older than my mother.

My mother never complained about this man, who loved her after his own fashion. She gave him two sons, my brothers Mohand and Lâmara. This man had a much younger brother who was childless. The latter wanted to draw up a deed whereby he bequeathed all his property to his wife. Before he could carry out this intention his elder brother set an ambush for him and the next day he was found dead against a haystack in an isolated spot outside the village known as *Sebala*, the place where all the villagers erected their haystacks. The murderer was never discovered and the case was filed and disposed of.

My mother told me that from that day her husband was under a curse. He was afflicted by a terrible disease: his whole body was covered with blisters, filled with liquid and this yellow liquid ran down his legs.

'The year of his death,' my mother said, 'there was a miraculous crop. In living memory the fig trees had never been loaded with so much fruit, the vines with such bunches of grapes, nor had such fine ears of corn ever been seen.

'When we went out to the fields, he would lift up the branches and say, "Look woman, look at all the good things God gives us!" And I would reply quietly, "*Ma ne der!*" (If we live long enough.)

'One day, when I answered him in these same words, he fell into a sudden rage and shook me, shouting, "We shall live, woman! We shall live!"

'He was not to see the figs ripen, nor the grapes. The crops had scarcely been gathered in, when he died.'

Her husband had not even been buried when my maternal uncle, Kaci Aïth-Lârbi-ou-Said, came to my mother and ordered her to leave her home. 'You and your children must come to live with us,' he insisted. 'Our mother will bring them up and you must marry again.'

'I shall stay with my children, in my own home,' she replied, thus defying her brother and the local customs. (These required a widow's children to return to the dead husband's family when they reach the age of seven, while she can choose either to live with her own parents or with her late husband's family while waiting to remarry.)

My uncle, who was very tall, seized a tile from the roof and threw it at her, fortunately missing. He went straight to the *tajmâat* (assembly place) and declared in the presence of witnesses, 'As from this day, I repudiate my sister Aïni. She is no longer a member of our family; whatever she does, whatever becomes of her, we dissociate ourselves from her fate. She is a stranger to us.'

He returned to his village and, from that day, my mother never saw her father's house again.

She saw to the burial of her husband, according to the tradition. With money that she borrowed in anticipation of her grape harvest, she bought a couple of oxen which she sacrificed for the repose of the soul of the deceased. The meat was divided among the whole village. Every family got a share, one portion per person. In addition a funeral banquet was served at the *tajmâat*, intended primarily for the poor who were thus able to feast on *couscous*.

My mother was left on her own at the age of twenty-two or twenty-three, with two children, the elder one five or six and the younger one three. She was very beautiful, with a clear pink complexion and blue-grey eyes, rather short and stocky, with broad shoulders, a strong chin and a low, obstinate forehead. She set to work bravely. She did the housework, fetched water, ground corn for the day, prepared her meals in the evening. During the day she worked in the fields.

When she needed a man's help she had to pay very dearly for it. In the winter, when the olives were ripe, she gave five days' work gathering the fallen fruit in return for one day's work from a thrasher.

But she was young and foolish. In her own courtyard there lived a young man from the same family as her old husband. She fell in love with him. And the inevitable happened. She became pregnant and the young man denied that he was the father of the child.

Kabyle customs are cruel. When a woman transgresses she must disappear, she must not be seen again. The family must not be sullied by her shame. Before the French rule, summary justice was practised: the relatives took the offender out into the fields, killed her and buried her under an embankment. But at that time, the French legal system was struggling to wipe out these brutal customs and this was my mother's salvation.*

When she was no longer able to hide her condition my brothers' uncles – the old husband's brothers – had a meeting. They decided to drive my mother out and take over the children whose property they coveted. When they tried to force her to leave, she went to the magistrates and laid a charge against them.

The magistrates came up to the village. The tribunal appointed a guardian and a deputy guardian for the children, drew up an inventory of my mother's property and left with the decree that no one must harm the widow or orphans.

On the night of my birth[†] my mother was all alone with her two small children: there was no one at hand to assist her or to go for help. She delivered herself and bit through the umbilical cord. The next day one old woman brought her a little food.

---

* Since 1874 French magistrates were the sole legal authorities for Muslims in Kabylia. In disputes relating to personal circumstances, as in this case, they took into account customary and Muslim law, while attempting to find a just and humane solution, even if, as may often happen, this was not in accordance with custom. For example, a woman who was not a virgin was recognised as having the right to dispose of her own person; custody of children was given to the mother; moreover, guardianship was arranged to prevent the spoliation of orphans. (See Jean-Paul Charnay, *La vie musulmane en Algérie d'après la jurisprudence de la première moitié du XXe siècle* (Muslim Life in Algeria, According to the Legal System in Force in the First Half of the Twentieth Century), Paris, P.U.F. 1965.

[†] Fadhma Aïth Mansour is presumed to have been born in 1882. See chronological table (D.S.B.).

When I was nine days old my mother tied me warmly to her breast, for it had been snowing, and set out, with a child in each hand, to lodge a complaint with the public prosecutor against my father. She wanted him to recognise me and give me his name. He refused because he was engaged to a girl from the village who came from a powerful family; they threatened to kill him if he abandoned this girl and he was afraid!

The case dragged on for three years. All this time, through heat and cold, my mother returned to plead and harass the magistrates. All the witnesses agreed that the man was indeed my father, for I was his living portrait. After three years he was sentenced to pay damages – the sum of 300 francs! – which my mother refused to accept, but since the law at that time forbade the establishment of paternity, he could not be forced to recognise me; so the seal of shame was branded on my forehead.

In despair, my mother plunged me into the icy waters of the spring. But I did not die.

My mother went about her usual tasks, night and day, with no assistance: washing, carding, combing, spinning and weaving her wool, ploughing her fields, gathering her figs, grapes, olives, doing her housework and cooking, sifting and grinding corn, barley, acorns, carting water, carrying wood.

When I was tiny, she left me sleeping until she returned; when I was a bit bigger she left a little pitcher of water next to me and a bowl containing a small portion of *couscous*.

When I woke up I picked at the grains of *couscous* with my fingers and when I had eaten it all I sucked the water out of the pitcher through its little spout. Then I went back to sleep until my mother's return. Sometimes, when she had to stay out late, a good-natured neighbour agreed to look after me for a short while, but this was rare.

The world is a cruel place and 'the child of sin' becomes the scapegoat of society, especially in Kabylia. I cannot count the blows I received. What endless bullying I suffered! If I ventured into the street, I would risk being knocked down and trampled upon.

The first picture that I can recall is of a summer's day, with a leaden sun beating down on a steep and dusty road; I see a lad of about ten driving some animals before him, and then a toddler, little more than a babe, all pink and white with fair, curly hair, running after him, screaming, '*D'hada! d'hada!*' (Big brother, big brother!) Then all is silence.

Then there immediately follows another picture: that of a house whose open door lets in a shaft of sunlight; in the sun, a woman bends over a naked child, whose body is covered with cactus spikes; hot tears fall on this bruised body from which the woman extricates the thorns, one by one.

I learned later that this child was me: I had followed my brother who was driving the oxen to the drinking trough and a vicious boy had pushed me into the hedge of prickly pears. My mother took fright. What was she to do with me? How was she to protect me from people's cruelty? She could not keep me shut up, but she was afraid that if I went out I would be killed and, in the eyes of the law, the blame would fall on her.

She heard that at Ouadhias there was a convent of the White Sisters, who took in little girls and looked after them. She thought that if she entrusted me to these nuns she would have no more worries on my account; no one would hurt me any more. Nevertheless, she held out for a long time as she loved me, I was her child. She had refused to give me to the magistrate's wife, who was childless and had wanted to adopt me after the incident of the cactus hedge, but seeing that I was still a victim of ill-treatment, she decided to take me to the White Sisters.

On Wednesday, market day, my mother lifted me on to her back and took me to Ouadhias. I have very little memory of this period of my life. Pictures, nothing but pictures. First, that of a very tall woman, dressed all in white, with black beads. Another object made of knotted rope hung next to the rosary – probably a whip; I learned later that she was the nun in charge of the little girls. There were other children with me, but all older, among these was Tassâdit Aïth Ouchen-Félicité, of whom I shall speak later.

According to my mother, I must have stayed for a year in this house – probably from the summer of 1885 to 1886. Every Wednesday, my mother came to see me; she would bring me the best things she had, hard-boiled eggs, girdle cake, pancakes, sweet white figs. So that the other children shouldn't take it out on me, she shared everything she brought amongst them all. Once a long time passed without a visit. Weeks went by. When I finally saw her again, she was pale and had lost weight. She explained that my brother Lâmara had had a fight with a boy of his own age; she had tried to separate them and the other child's father had thrown a stone at her which had hit her on the forehead. She had been carried home unconscious. Her life had been in danger for several days, but she had recovered, and she lifted my little hand to her head, so that I could feel the hole there.

From this whole period of my life, I can only recall the tune of *Ave Maria Stella* and the impression of the chapel, all lit up, with the officiating priest holding out the monstrance. (For a long time after I had left Ouadhias, I wondered what all that meant.) But, most of all, I am haunted by a terrible picture: that of a tiny girl standing against the wall of a corridor: the child is covered with filth, dressed in sackcloth, with a little mug full of excrement hung around her neck. She is crying. A priest is walking towards her; the nun who is with him explains that she is a wicked little girl who has thrown her comrades' thimbles into the privy and so has been made to climb down into it to retrieve them: she is covered with the contents of the cesspool, which also fill the mug.

In addition to this punishment, the child was also flogged till she bled: when my mother came the following Wednesday, she found me still covered with the marks from the whip. She stroked my bruises, then sent for the nun and, pointing to the weals, she said, 'Was it for this that I entrusted my daughter to you? Give her back to me!' The nun undressed me, even stripping me of my chemise. My mother took off her headscarf, knotted two corners together over my shoulder, pinned the material together on the other shoulder with a large thorn, by way of a clasp, untied her wide woollen girdle which she fastened round her head, and lifted me on to her back.

And so I left the Sisters of Ouadhias.

While I was at Ouadhias, a man from the village had asked my mother to marry him; he was not from our clan; he was young and strong and promised to support her and her children; my mother agreed, as my brothers were not yet able to defend her or indeed to look after themselves.

This man went to see my mother's family, taking the bride-price, but my uncle Kaci refused the money, saying he no longer had a sister. So my mother remarried, but she wouldn't go to live with her husband's family, who in any case would not have accepted her.*

Her brothers tried once again to drive my mother out and to take over her children and her property; and once again she had to go to the law. She had the last word: she kept her home, her children and the man who had taken on the burden of marrying her and protecting her.

He kept his word until the day when his elder brother died, and he had to take this man's place in looking after his own family: his elderly father, his mother and his brother's widow.† A little girl was born from my mother's second marriage, inheriting my mother's lovely blue-grey eyes.

My mother was a stout-hearted woman. She was in the habit of saying, '*Tichert-iou-khir-t'mira guergazen*' (The tatooing on my chin is worth more than a man's beard!) And it was true. I only saw my mother weep twice: when I was thrown into the cactus hedge and when she heard of her own mother's death. The thing that grieved her most was to be separated for ever from her family. Half-way between Taourirth-Moussa-ou-Amar and Tizi-Hibel there was a stream where the women went to do their washing, near the hamlet of Tagragra. Every Wednesday, on market day, my mother would meet my grandmother there. They would each bring some delicacy to offer to the other. But one morning my grandmother did not turn up; a neighbour told my mother that her mother had died during the night. The whole day my mother waited outside the house while acquaintances pleaded with my uncle Kaci to let her come in and say her last farewell to the dead woman; my uncle Kaci was adamant. My mother came home broken-hearted. I was at home at the time as it was the holiday to

---

* In a normal marriage, the wife joins the husband's family. It is rare for a young couple to be cut off from the family community on both sides.
† In cases where the father is no longer able to take full responsibility for the family, owing to extreme age, or in the event of his death, the eldest son must take charge. If the eldest son dies, the next one succeeds him, and must carry his duty to the extent of marrying his brother's widow.

celebrate the feast of the sheep, which fell that year during the summer, and my little sister and I were witness to her despair, without understanding what it was about, but the memory is still vivid . . .

In the autumn, the *kaïd* sent for my mother and said, 'Your daughter Fadhma is a burden to you, take her to Fort-National where a school for girls has just been opened, she will be happy and treated well, and the Administrator will take her under his wing. You will have nothing more to fear from your first husband's brothers.' My mother held out for a long time, but her young husband, as well as the village people, who still considered me the child of sin, were disapproving. In October or November 1886, she agreed to give me up. Once again she took me on her back and we set out. I cannot recall this journey; I can only remember that as we climbed down towards the river we picked arbutus berries to eat – I can still see the red fruit. This brings us to the end of the first part of my childhood. I returned to the village from time to time, for the holidays, but I was never illtreated again.

Taddert-ou-Fella

The orphanage of Taddert-ou-Fella, which owes its name to the nearby village, was founded between 1882 and 1884. At this same time, the first schools in Greater Kabylia were opened, one in Beni-Yenni, with M. Verdy in charge, one in Tamazirth, under M. Gorde, and one in Tizi-Rached under M. Maille.*

M. and Mme Malaval ran the Fort-National school. The then Administrator, M. Sabatier, wanted to start a school for girls and Mme Malaval agreed to take charge of this.

He summoned all the *kaïds*, cavalrymen and rural police in his area and asked them to ride through the *douars* (villages) and collect as

* For boys only (D.S.B.).

many girls as possible. The *kaïds* and the horsemen set off, with the rural police, who set the example by bringing their own daughters. There were girls of all ages: some already adolescents and some still toddlers. Soon the premises at the Fort were inadequate, so the commune built the school at Taddert-ou-Fella.

There was a turning on the road to Mekla, just over a mile from Fort-National; above this turning there was a stretch of ground in the shape of a basin, surrounded by hills and with streams running down to the right and left, bounded to the south by the road and to the north by a hill, on the top of which stood a ruined house. The Kabyle village was perched on the hillside about half a mile further on.

In 1890 a sign could still be seen at the side of the road, on which was written, *Orphanage of Taddert-ou-Fella. No admission without authorisation*. Since then, the post on which this notice was fixed has fallen down and it has never been replaced.

When I arrived at the school I was still very young and I cannot remember much of my first two years there. I was very impressed when I was taken to the headmistress. My mother had first gone to see the Adminstrator to put me in his care. This wasn't M. Sabatier, who had been elected Deputy, but his successor, M. Demonque. The commune was still responsible for the school expenses. I saw a tall woman, dressed all in black; she seemed terribly sad to me. She had recently lost her only son from typhoid and her husband had died some little time before. They came from Aveyron where they had been ruined when phylloxera destroyed all the vines. Since the death of her husband and son, Mme Malaval had devoted herself wholeheartedly to her school.

I can remember an immense room with a wooden roof where you could see the beams, like in a stable; there were wide, high windows on three sides and the headmistress's quarters were built up against the fourth side. This room contained three rows of beds made of three planks on trestles; there were two grey blankets for sleeping, no pillow or sheets either.

When I arrived the dormitory was full. There were some really big girls who were put in charge of the smaller ones. My memories are vague up to 1888. In October of that year, I was put up into the big girls' class: there were four of us little ones: Alice, Inès, Blanche and myself, Marguerite. We had all been given French names, as there were too many Fadhmas, Tassâdits and Dabhias. Up till then I had been in Mlle Soulé's class where we had learnt such pretty songs like 'The Bengali' and 'Dame Tartine'. After M. Sabatier left, the *Kaïds* and the local police stopped their propaganda. The big girls, who were really too old for school, went home to get married and were never replaced. Soon the dormitory was too big and had to be divided into two, with one part to be used as a refectory and classroom. In fact, some classrooms which had been built on the hill when the school had its maximum complement, later had to be closed. In any case, it was not very convenient in the cold weather to have to climb up and down the steep paths to go to lessons or meals.

I shall say nothing of all the girls who passed through the school while I was there, for I have little to tell. I lived for years among them, without feeling affection or dislike for any of them: we did our lessons, we ate, we slept. As far as the food was concerned, it was the same as in all poor boarding-schools: black coffee for breakfast, with a piece of bread; for our midday meal, lentils full of grit, haricot beans, rice or split peas, with very little in the way of green vegetables, except for the wild salads that we picked when we went for walks in the fields. Later, however, I can remember winter evenings, by the fire in the semi-darkness, and the big girls who knew wonderful tales: we huddled round these story-tellers after our evening soup, until the teacher came to send us to bed.

There were also games that we played, running around wildly to get warm, while we sang 'Auprès de ma blonde', and 'Anne of Brittany in her clogs'. And there were walks when we had been good: every afternoon, if it was fine, we went as far as 'the red turning' until it was time for lessons to begin again.

'The red turning' was on the road to Mekla. The bank overhanging the road was completely red – I don't know if it was the rock which gave it this colour. Some of us stayed below the road, others climbed up a dozen or so feet to reach a rough area, covered with fallen rocks, where magnificent cyclamens grew. At other times we took the road towards Fort-National. The graphic memory of these walks, on spring or summer evenings, is still with me. I shall never forget the sight of the trees covered with wild roses or clematis that we made into garlands, and the sweet-scented honeysuckle, the carpets of yellow and white daisies, the cornflowers and buttercups. I have never since that time seen so many flowers or such a lovely scene.

On Sundays and Thursdays we went for other longer walks along the Djurdjurda road: sometimes we went as far as the iron spring, taking a piece of dry bread to eat. At other times we went into the 'Arts and Crafts Centre' – a large building that the Kabyles had burnt down in 1871 and of which only the cellars and some smoke-blackened walls remained. On the way there we passed through the town of Fort-National; on the way back we went round outside the ramparts and ended up in the garden of the barracks. The branches of the chestnut trees formed an arch over the road and sometimes we found a chestnut, nestling inside its burr, like a sea-urchin.

But the thing that has left me with my best memories is the stream! 'My stream', I called it, as every year for ten years, from October when we returned to school, until the beginning of July, when we left for the holidays, not one day passed without my visiting my stream, at least once, sometimes even several times a day. It was my refuge! The stream ran down for nearly a mile on the right-hand side of the school grounds, from its source amidst the rocks a little higher up. In summer it was a gentle little trickle of water, flowing quietly between its banks which sloped gently down on our side but were quite steep on the other. It was a stiff climb to reach the field belonging to Fatimat-Hamou, our neighbour. That's where I would go to pick wild cherries, figs, ears of corn, anything edible for an afternoon snack, especially wild onions.

Tall poplars grew along the banks, covered with vines from which bunches of golden grapes hung over the water. These grapes did not ripen till November. When the owners came to pick them, while I was in school, they dropped a few pale, juicy fruit into the transparent stream, and when lessons were over, at four o'clock, I would go and collect them and give myself a treat.

In winter the stream became a torrent and at night, when it rained, we could hear it roaring.

As it cascaded down it formed a natural pool, which filled up with foaming water. My stream! I cannot count the happy hours I spent beside you, picking countless violets and buttercups, not to mention

Fatima-t-Hamou's plums, which I hid in the hay till they'd finished ripening!

The school was reached from the road by a gravel path which ran through fields of fig trees; these were bounded on one side by the stream, and on the other by the track which led up to the village, half-way between Taddert-ou-Fella and the school.

There was also the boys' school, on the other side of which ran a brook, overhung with oak trees. I would return from a walk there with my pockets full of acorns. Still further on, there was a tangle of undergrowth: brambles, hawthorns, broom and bracken. In autumn the brambles were covered with blackberries, but best of all were the hawthorn bushes with their white flowers in spring and their red berries, which we called *zârour*, in autumn. On the other side of the stream was the house belonging to Mohand Akhli, the man who worked at the school when I first got there; his field sloped down to the water where there was a bed of reeds and this miraculous spring, lukewarm in winter and ice-cold in summer. In summer, when the water at school was always too warm, we used to go and fill bottles at Mohand Akhli's spring.

I lived like this for ten years, more often out of doors than in, except when rain kept me indoors, or it was time for lessons.

The winters were very cold and it often snowed for weeks on end. The snow was so deep that the servant couldn't go to fetch provisions, especially bread that he normally brought every morning. So we ate bread that was a week old, as he'd have had to dig his way out to get to the road.

So, another of my memories is of the snow 'falling like fleece' as they say in the Kabyle language, and of icicles, like huge candles, breaking loose from the tiles and falling with a dull thud into this soft woolly mass. As soon as the snow stopped, we would run outside and run races over the white surface. We made snowmen and threw snowballs. In the classroom we had a fire roaring in the stove, with a pan full of melting ice standing on it.

Then we would dash to try to be the first back so as to get a good seat near the fire; those with the least inhibitions always got the best places. There was one girl named Yamina, who we called Germaine; she was strong and pushy and if she didn't get the seat she wanted, she grabbed the child who was in it and deposited her on the floor.

The nights were the worst. It was cold and there was nothing for the boarders to pee into, so several of the little ones wet their beds. This happened to me. I can still recall how terrified I was when two of the big girls picked me up, one by the feet, the other by the arms, carried me outside to the washplace (there were none inside the building) and doused me under the cold tap. We were kept under the stream of ice-cold water for several minutes, which seemed like an eternity. Then we were energetically rubbed dry. I don't know who had recommended this cure, but it worked like a charm, and I never did pee in my bed again.

When I arrived, the boys' school was run by a Frenchman and his sister; they took classes during the day and returned every evening to the old house up the hill to eat and sleep.

Sometimes they came to visit us, but one day the brother vomited up blood and they both went away and never came back.

For a long time the school at Taddert-ou-Fella was considered a show-place and we were visited by a succession of members of the French government, including Jules Ferry, and often tourists came simply out of curiosity, like the Grand Duke George of Russia.

When I was small I was never afraid of anything, and when the class was asked questions, I was always the one who answered. And when we had to ask a teacher or the headmistress something, I always volunteered to do it.

My mother did come to see me, but not as often as to Ouadhias, as the distance was much greater, but as soon as my brothers were big enough, they always came on feast days, to bring me my share of good things.

For some years, until 1890, I did not go back to my village, as the holidays were too short and my brothers not big enough to come and fetch me. That is why I used to go for the Aïd holiday to one or other of my school-friends whose parents lived close by. In Kabylia hospitality knows no limits and, however poor people are, they never refuse a child a piece of *galette* or a dish of *couscous*.

I did not see my mother's house and our village again until 1890 or '91. My brothers were finally old enough to look after their own property; they could also go to market to sell the produce from their fields and the *burnouses* (hooded cloaks) that my mother wove. She told me later how delighted she was when she no longer had to rely on strangers for these transactions.

As I have already mentioned, her second husband had left her, to take the place of his dead brother in his own family, according to the Kabyle demands of *kif*, honour. My mother never saw him again, but she never had a bad word to say against him, as he had helped her through a very difficult period. My little sister had died of smallpox the preceding winter.

I set off for home with Alice, a school-friend who lived in a village near ours; old Ali-ou-Idhir escorted us as the teachers wanted to take their holidays with us all out of the way. This short holiday passed without incident; no one dared interfere with me any more, but I rarely left the house. Then I went back to school.

That year it snowed very heavily. We were snowbound for weeks. A number of little girls came to ask us to take them in; some of them were the daughters of beggar-women from the Aïth-Khelili tribe, but they still managed to bring the children extra delicacies to eat. There was one family of orphans who came to us, whose mother had burnt to death and whose father had been murdered on the way back from selling fritters at the market. There were five of them, four girls and a boy; the two eldest girls were more or less my age, the third one was younger and the littlest one couldn't walk yet.

There were also some French girls among the boarders, daughters of colonists or café owners, from Mekla, Tizi-Ouzou and Fort-National. They had a separate dormitory and dining-room. Some of them left school to get married, some to go to other schools. I didn't get to know all of them. The last one, a colonist's daughter from Mekla, became a primary school teacher after getting her teaching diploma. Another of the pupils was appointed to teach in Azrou-ou-Quellal. Several of them obtained their school-leaving certificate. The big ones had all left, except three who were entered for the diploma but who were all failed, as if on purpose.

The years went by, the seasons, summers and winters. In 1892 I in turn passed my school certificate. I was fairly good at the subjects I liked. I was top in French history, but I hated geography – I could never remember all the Departments and Districts, whereas I can still remember in detail all the kings of France, who married whom, who succeeded whom, and all about the French Revolution and the Napoleonic era. I loved French, except when I had to explain proverbs and maxims. What I liked best was to make up stories. I wasn't bad at arithmetic.

Every year we received bales of blue and white check gingham to make our dresses; once or twice, in winter, we had rough brown dresses. In the autumn the shoemaker came to fit us for clogs, and sometimes shoes. When they were worn out they were never repaired, we just threw them away, chanting: 'Now my shoes let in the rain, Mister Chagrau is to blame!' (That was the name of the shoemaker.) So our lives passed peacefully until 1893. That was the time when the Administrator, M. Demonque, was transferred to Sidi-Bel-Abbas as Sub-Prefect, and was replaced by M. Masselot. Meanwhile one of our pupils obtained her school-leaving certificate and was appointed to the post of primary school teacher in Aït-Hichem, the only Kabyle village where the *Kaïd* had set up a mixed school for boys and girls, and to set an example he sent his own daughter, who eventually became a pupil-teacher there.

The teacher at the Aït-Hichem school soon got to know a young man from her own village who had himself just left the normal college in Bouzareah. He had been appointed to the school in Taddert-ou-Fella to replace the previous teacher, who had had to leave for health reasons. The young couple wanted to marry but their parents refused their consent as the two families were enemies. Mme Malaval took the matter up and appealed to the Chamber of Deputies. They won their case and so became the first Kabyle married couple both to be school teachers. It caused a scandal, known at the time as 'the case of the beautiful Fatma'. This did the school a great deal of harm, I think, and created a number of enemies for the headmistress among people who were jealous of her success. People were beginning to demand the emancipation of Muslim women. At that time school was compulsory for boys; if a pupil played truant, the father and son were sentenced to three days in prison and a fine of fifteen francs. So boys attended school regularly. But, alas! nothing similar was enforced for girls. There was no secular teaching for them, with the exception of our school which unfortunately soon had to close.

In fact, M. Masselot came to see us and told us that the commune could not bear the costs of the orphanage any longer, so the school must close and the pupils be sent back to their families. He had us stand in rows before him and said, 'I can't help you. If you were men I'd issue you with a *burnouse* and give you a job in the police or the horse regiment, but you are girls . . . ' And he added casually, 'They're pretty, they'll get married . . . !'

Mme Malaval refused to obey; she kept the orphanage going for six months out of her own savings; she moved heaven and earth, writing to members of the government and any influential persons who might help her. Eventually she got her way in 1893. It was decided that the Taddert-ou-Fella Orphanage should be taken over by the State and re-named 'The Taddert-ou-Fella Normal School'.

The Normal School

We became a Normal School in 1893. Certain changes were intro-duced; we had qualified teachers from the teacher training college in Miliana. We were better fed but pupils who were considered incap-able of benefiting from the teaching were sent home. To ensure the future of our establishment, we had to have primary schools, but the Kabyles were more adamant than ever in their refusal to send their daughters to school. Still, Mme Malaval did found a few infant schools in some villages but there were no girls sufficiently qualified to take charge of them, so she had to appoint some of her former pupils who had passed their school certificate; even then only boys attended these schools. Mme Malaval went to inspect them every three months. Examiners came to our Normal School in Taddert-ou-Fella to supervise the school certificate exam. A few girls passed. The others were sent home.

Things went on in this way for a further two years.

In 1895 four or five of us took the examination for the elementary diploma. Although at least one of us was very well prepared, we all failed.

To travel to Algiers for the exam, we had dressed in regional costume that is worn for important feast days, that is, a silk *fouta* with sash and headscarf. We were too conspicuous: the Kabyles and all the orthodox Muslims made a scandal. The school was closed once more.

When the headmistress announced that we all had to go back to our villages many of the girls rebelled; they even wrote to the Englishwomen* to ask if they would take them, but they got no reply.

My heart was heavy as I set off for home, for although I was still very young adversity had made me older than my years and I knew I had only more suffering to look forward to, but there was nothing I could do about it.

My brother came to fetch me with the donkey to carry the little tin trunk that contained my modest wardrobe.

I spent my time as I had always done in the past, whenever I went home for the holidays. My mother went out to the fields; she picked the figs and dried them; my brothers took it in turns to bring in sackfuls of ash leaves to feed the oxen and the other animals; they carried the basketfuls of figs and grapes.

In recent years I had begun to read widely. Everything that I could lay my hands on. Since the school had been promoted to the status of Normal School we had had a library with a good stock of all the books that were popular at the time. We had read Alphonse Daudet's *Lettres de mon moulin*, François Coppée's poems, *Le Pêcheur d'Islande* by Pierre Loti and Victor Hugo's *Bug-Jargal* and *Quatre-Vingt-Treize*. We had studied Molière, Racine and La Fontaine.

Now, when the heat outside was stifling, I closed the door of the house and sat in the dark, going over in my head everything I had read, until my mother came home at nightfall. Sometimes I went with her to the fields, but the sharp stubble hurt my bare feet too much.

I often went to sit beside the spring in the shade of the vines; the grapes hung from the branches in heavy red and white bunches, and

* The reference is probably to a Methodist mission, as there were some in Kabylia.

on the hill, in the distance, I could make out Fort-National, surrounded by its white ramparts and red-tiled roofs. I re-lived all the
journeys I had made there and back, all the weariness, all the discom-
fort I had experienced!

How often I said to my mother, on the eve of my return to school,
'You must wake me very early so that I can reach the hill up to Aït-
Frah before the sun gets too hot.' That hill was so steep for my little
legs! You always had to climb to get to Fort-National from our village. 'Whichever way you approach Fort-National, it's always
uphill,' says the proverb.

And every time it was downhill as far as the river while it was still
cool. Then the easy part of the journey finished. Immediately after
that the sun started beating down mercilessly on the back of my head.
Sometimes I had to run to keep up with my brother who walked faster
than me.

I also saw myself setting off with my friend Alice and her father
who was a village policeman and had a mule; the two of them rode on
the mule and I had to follow on foot.

Most of all I thought about the walk from Fort-National to Taddert-
ou-Fella along the road that I loved with its wild roses, clematis and
sweet-scented honeysuckle! There would be no more walks to the
stream – *my* stream. I would never see all that again . . . And I smarted
with longing for my lost paradise. I leaned my head against the vine
and day-dreamed, wondering anxiously whatever was to become
of me.

I fed on figs and grapes. When my mother and brothers had finished
their hard day's work we all climbed back up to the village where we
slept till midnight. Then my eldest brother came back with his load of
ash leaves; hidden deep in the load there were treasures: heavy
bunches of golden grapes or vegetables from our patch: long green
beans, little squashes, sometimes even juicy red plums. Then my
mother set to work to grind the grain for the next day's food.

And I shut my eyes and re-lived my childhood, as far back as I
could remember.

First, when I was quite tiny, with a girl called Micha, who carried me
on her back to comfort me when I cried for my mother.

Later, walks by moonlight. And going to watch and listen from a distance to the dancing on 14 July. On one occasion I fell asleep and rolled down the slope and narrowly escaped a serious accident.

Carnival time when the big girls made a guy out of wrapping paper. They carried it round the grounds and we followed, chanting, 'Goodbye, Carnival! You're leaving us, you're on your way!' And in the evening we poured paraffin over the guy and set fire to it outside the dormitory.

On fine May evenings we used to go to listen to the congregation singing hymns to the Virgin Mary and we learned to sing with them,

> Of Mary, let us all proclaim
> Her glory and her greatness,

and also,

> This is the month of Mary
> This is the fairest month!

I was even moved by the memory of the times I was punished by being shut up in the dark, or of the occasional clouts over the head I received. Then there were the summer nights when I was eaten alive by bedbugs, so I dipped my nightgown in the washbasin and put it on again soaking wet, thinking, 'That'll keep the bugs away so I'll be able to get some sleep!'

These unhappy memories faded as I thought of the times I walked down to my little stream and back, and of the evenings I spent on its banks, in the shade of the linden trees, reading a book . . . that I had purloined!

There were also the days when we had no school and I went off to different places, as my own home was too far away.

One year, I spent the New Year holiday in Tizi-Rached, where I went with Germaine and Charlotte. This village lies in a valley, hidden beneath olive groves and it rarely snows there. When the holidays were over we had to go back to school. We set off one Sunday in bright sunshine, but when we got half-way we found the road blocked with snow. The further we went, the deeper the snow-drifts were.

Finally, we lost the track altogether and some of the girls with me wanted to turn back but I refused to follow them, so they were forced to go on, keeping to the banks of the stream where there was no snow. We didn't get back till one o'clock in the afternoon, worn out and starving. The headmistress was there to receive us and make us change our clothes and go to bed to get warm.

I can still see this woman quite clearly in my mind's eye. She was tall with broad shoulders and a rather masculine appearance, a broad, intelligent forehead, piercing grey eyes in a long face, with a determined chin. She had quite a large, slightly snub nose, a fairly big mouth with very beautiful teeth. Her brown hair was very long and when worn in a plait it fell well below her waist. We sometimes saw her in her dressing-gown. I can still see her explaining a lesson to us, when I couldn't take my eyes off her. She would walk up and down in front of us, and she would teach us patriotic songs. She only cared passionately about two things: France and her school, as this was all she had after both her husband and her son died on Algerian soil.

Sometimes she talked to us about her family who came from the Aveyron region. She was really quite well-connected and had received a solid education at the best convent in Rodez, from where her former teacher, Sister Saint-Charles, still wrote to her.

She was a sincere believer, but she never mentioned her religion to us as the school was supposed to be non-sectarian. She went to mass whenever she could, as the school was about one and a half miles from the town.

She taught us to sew and knit. The big girls especially learned to do very fine needlework and they made her the most beautiful underwear as a surprise for her birthday – nightdresses, camisoles, or drawers, with tiny pleats or embroidered with herringbone stitch or with lace. I was too young and I had neither the patience nor the inclination for this sort of work.

I recalled all these memories most vividly during these summer evenings of 1895.

When my mother finished grinding the corn for the following day, she collected the flour in a little basket and lay down at last beside me to rest.

For the last few years she had been very devout. She had gone to see a well-known *sheikh* who had given her a rosary and whenever she had a moment free she would pray. She never said a bad word.

Every morning she was up before dawn and went to the spring to fill the two water jars for the mosques – one at each end of the village – so that the faithful who came to pray could perform their ablutions. When that was done, she went to fetch fresh water for our own domestic use, carrying several full pitchers on her back.

When she got home I was still asleep. She lit the fire and made enough *galettes* to last the day; she gave some to my brothers with a drink of whey and then they went off to the fields.

When I woke up I found my share put aside with a basket of fresh figs which my brother had brought back during the night.

My mother had done all her work: she had cleared out the animals' shed and taken the manure out to the field that we owned near the village and had gone off to pick figs before it got too hot.

That was when my brothers also came home and they wouldn't go back to the fields until the heat had abated. This time I went with them, to sit beside the spring.

They gathered the figs and laid them out one by one on reed trays. They had made a little shelter out of branches, under the tallest ash, where they took it in turns to sleep to keep thieves away.

We picked the tender green beans, courgettes and leaves of the young onions from our vegetable patch and when my mother got back in the evening she made the *mekfoul* – steamed vegetables covered with *couscous*. When it was ready, she turned the whole lot out on to the big dish that she had used to roll out the *couscous* and sprinkled it with virgin olive oil; she stirred the mixture with two wooden spoons and we set to. Anything left over was kept for the one who left earliest the following morning for the fields.

On Wednesdays one of my brothers went to market and brought meat back. That was the only thing we had to buy; otherwise we lived exclusively on the produce from our own property.

I had spent every school holiday in this way. Already most of the figs had been picked and brought into the house, where they took up most of the room. August was over, we were well into September. I was not unhappy; my mother and brothers left me alone, but I kept thinking, 'What am I going to do? What will become of me? How long can I stay in this house?' My eldest brother was engaged and would soon be married.

When my mother was out I sometimes went round to a neighbour's. They were all very helpful as now and again I would rock a baby to sleep for them. One old woman with a pleasant face, in spite of eyelids all inflamed from some disease, used to say, 'May God make the sun shine out for you from behind the clouds!' And I would answer 'Amen!'

Towards the end of September I unexpectedly received a letter from Mme Malaval, inviting me to return to school. What a joy that was! What a release!

On 30 September my brother went to market and brought back meat so that I could have a good meal before I left. I packed all my things in my tin trunk and asked mother to wake me before daybreak, while the stars were still out. I set off very early. Mother was sad; she had grown accustomed to having me at home and having the house well guarded when she was obliged to be out. She embraced me affectionately and wished me '*bon voyage*'.

So I took the familiar road once more, covering the part downhill while it was still cool, but as usual the sun beat down eventually on the back of my head and it was impossible to find any shade.

On I went happily along the road from the Fort to my school. It was still full of flowers but the leaves were beginning to turn yellow, the festoons of honeysuckle and clematis would soon be withered. Nevertheless I looked with delight on all these things that I had never thought to see again.

It was still early when I reached school – not quite nine o'clock. A few girls had arrived before me, others turned up in the course of the morning, some did not come back at all.

There were, I think, seven or eight of us altogether: Charlotte, Alice, Inès and myself, as well as Renée, Maria and Juliette. So I realised how precarious the situation was: there were no teachers except for Mme Malaval . . .

There was a new servant, the former one having gone to Mekla to look after a few plots of land and a four- or five-roomed house.

Mme Malaval had bought a small property and had moved all her personal possessions there. The new servant ran errands and even did the cooking. I can't say how many days we remained idle, waiting for something to happen – we weren't sure what.

I resumed my walks down to the stream. I sometimes went as far as the old abandoned house. I wandered from one place to another like a soul in torment. Then we were sent away again for a short time. There had not been time to warn my family to come and fetch me so Mme Malaval sent me to Mekla to stay with her manager. I set off with Juliette and her brother who were going to Aïth-Khelili.

Mme Malaval thought we'd only be away for a few days. She even said so to a family of schoolteachers she knew, the Girardots.

I can't remember exactly how long I stayed in Mekla. The family I was with consisted of husband and wife (a former pupil of my school) and their two children. The husband's brother and sister also lived with them; the latter was so ugly, I can't even begin to describe her – at school we used to call her 'the Chinawoman'. The brother was mentally deficient, just about able – at a pinch – to look after the sheep.

I tried to make myself useful; I ate the same food as they did.

The house had only one room and the figs happened to be stored there after they had been gathered, so sometimes, when I was hungry, I helped myself to one. But the ones I took came from the headmistress's share of the crop, so I wasn't robbing my hosts.

It was well into the autumn and ploughing had begun. M. Ou Hamitouche, the manager, had taken on a *khammès* whose wife made a large jar out of clay and straw to store the grain in (this was called an *akhoufi*).

The day ploughing began she made a dish known locally as *abissar* – a coarse wheaten *couscous* with plenty of haricot beans.

Day after day passed. I looked after the youngest child when its mother was busy; I rocked the cradle and sang it to sleep. I lay on the bare earth, under the cradle, re-living my past existence, still anxiously wondering what would become of me. But youth is optimistic and I did not lose hope.

All these memories filled me with nostalgia. Many things which I had forgotten now came back to mind. First the long journeys by mule to Aït-Hichem, to visit the former pupil who was now the teacher at the primary school there. It was winter, during the January holidays, I think. There were snow-drifts on either side of the road through which we had to dig our way with picks and shovels and, seated on the backs of the mules, we could touch the snow with our feet.

I also recalled the day the Minister for Education was supposed to come to visit the school. The big girls went out to pick branches of foliage in the ravine to make a triumphal arch to welcome him, but he never turned up.

We went as far as Fort-National to meet him, wearing unmatched rope-soled sandals and we came back drenched.

I thought of the semolina *couscous* served on Sundays, that the big girls delighted in rolling out; they made *afdir-ou-qessoul* with the grain left over – a sort of pancake cooked in sauce that we ate together in the big dish that the *couscous* had been rolled in.

So, as I rocked the baby in its cradle and lulled it to sleep, I lulled my own anxiety and distress.

I also went with my hosts to the wash-place.

And that is about all I can remember.

The days went by, each one as uneventful as the last and I continued to live in the past and fear of the future. Just at that time, I had a dream which I later came to look on as prophetic.

I was in a deep ravine through which clear water ran and on both sides, to the right and left, I could see two walls of smooth ice. I tried in vain to climb up these walls.

As all my efforts were unsuccessful, I lay down beside the stream, no doubt waiting to die. Suddenly I saw a huge bird hovering with outstretched wings above my head. I watched terror-struck as it wheeled around. Finally, I saw it plunge down towards me out of the clouds and then it lifted me up. I don't know how long I was borne up on its wings; it flew over many villages, many rivers and finally deposited me on a plateau where the Michelet hospital stood with its arcades. Then I woke up.

I didn't understand my dream till much later; it was in this hospital that my destiny was to be realised.

A few weeks later I received a message from Mme Malaval, telling me to leave with Juliette, whose brother would take us back to school.

Juliette arrived the next day. She seemed as miserable as I was delighted.

So I saw my beloved school once more. When I got there I found it practically deserted; the few pupils who were still going to attend, however, returned one by one.

Mme Malaval was very dejected. She had offered to resign if she was the cause of the authorities wanting to close the school, and the Director of Education had accepted her sacrifice. Another woman had been appointed to run the school.

We waited for several weeks, a month perhaps. We started lessons again, dictations, arithmetic problems, as if nothing had changed. Then one day Mme Malaval told us that the new head was on her way. This separation was a great wrench for all of us, but especially for her, as I didn't realise till much later how much she had given up.

We wept as we said goodbye to her. I never saw her again. I never heard of her again. Except once. I don't know if it was in the spring of 1896 or '97. She had come back to see us but the new head, Mme Sahuc, kept us shut up in the classroom while she received her, and it wasn't till she had gone that we heard of her visit. She tried to see M. Combes, the then Minister for Education, when he came to Algeria for an inspection, but it appears that he refused to receive her.

M. Combes came to the school, congratulated Mme Sahuc on our appearance and promised us each ten francs and a huswife. But on his return to Paris he was run over and we are still waiting for his huswife!

Mme Sahuc had studied at Miliana and had apparently applied for a lectureship. She considered Taddert-ou-Fella as a last resort. She – or rather her husband – came from Blidah, where he had some property. He visited his wife from time to time, but mostly lived on his farm.

As soon as I saw her, I knew instinctively that I would never like her. The way she had behaved towards my first headmistress infuriated me, and I never forgave her for not having let us say goodbye to her for the last time.

For that was the last that I ever heard of Mme Malaval. I did not know her address and I was never able to get in touch with her; but in my heart of hearts I have always worshipped her, I really loved her and her memory has always been nearly sacred to me.

We resumed our daily routine; we had a woman to do the cooking, a boy for the shopping and errands and an assistant teacher to help Mme Sahuc. But I think she had received instructions that we were not to be educated in the same way any longer: we were not to be trained to become primary school teachers.

She sent the boy to buy wool which she had washed, so that we could learn to spin and weave, as she told us. There were some girls who had a taste for this and produced beautiful wool, but for some reason I disliked this work.

We hardly had any proper lessons and we were not entered for any exams. Whenever I had a moment free I escaped to my stream, which was only a few yards from the school. I gazed on the carpets of buttercups and daisies again; and there were other flowers as well, like little blue eyes. The hawthorn flowered once more in the hedgerows and the brambles were laden with blackberries. I went back to the oakwoods where I used to fill my pockets with acorns when I was small and always hungry. Now we were no longer hungry, but the atmosphere was unbearable and I personally felt that everything I had loved was coming to an end . . . Nevertheless things dragged on till July 1897.

We felt very unsettled throughout that year. The girls chatted among themselves about this and that. The rug that had been set up to be woven on the loom was finished, not particularly well. Two girls had been expelled for fighting at night. And I, for my part, was storing up more memories.

I climbed up the two paths again: the one on the right, winding up gently, used to be reserved for the teachers; the path on the left leading straight as a ladder up the steep slope, was the one the pupils were supposed to use. Now we were free to take either path!

Since then, I have often thought of the freezing mornings when we got up before daybreak and had to climb these paths to prepare our lessons, by the light of a smoking lamp. What good had all this trouble been, I wondered, what was the good of all this misery? What use would it all be now?

Now I roamed through these big, empty classrooms in which my childhood had been spent. I gazed at all the illustrations from La Fontaine's *Fables* that covered the walls: *The Heron*, *The Wolf and the Stork*, *The Fox and the Goat*, *The Child and the Schoolmaster*. I had learned all these fables off by heart. For ten years I had sat on these benches. What use had it been to me?

In the summer of 1897 I was ill; I ran a very high temperature, the result, I think, of sunstroke. I had to stay in bed for more than two weeks, and I can still feel the impression of my heart beating against the wooden planks of the bed. Mme Sahuc never came near me, she never brought me a single infusion, and when I begged the other girls to make less noise, she said, 'You'll have to get used to suffering!' Dahbia-Maria was the only one who came to ask me if I needed anything. I asked her to soak my handkerchief in vinegar, it deadened the throbbing in my head and I could doze off to sleep. After two weeks I did at least get a quinine tablet. When I was able to get up, I was very weak and only gradually managed to resume normal life. At the end of June we were told to start packing up as we had to go back home at the beginning of July. The school was going to be closed down for good.

The inspector who had said, 'They're not bad-looking, they'll get married,' did not know that the Kabyle man instinctively mistrusted an educated woman.

My brother came to fetch me at the beginning of July. I bade farewell to the whole school and its surroundings and paid a last visit to my stream, only this year, because of my illness, I had not stolen any of Fatima-t-Hamou's plums or pears. I said goodbye to the oaks and the fig trees, to the classrooms and the dormitory with the beds made from three planks. I paused once more before the illustrations from La Fontaine's *Fables*, which covered the walls, at the wash place where I had been doused so often, and all the unchanging nature which had witnessed my countless sorrows and rare joys. I said farewell for ever to Taddert-ou-Fella. I kissed my fellow pupils, said a curt goodbye to Mme Sahuc and turned my back on my childhood and adolescence.

Memories of my Village

When I set off with my brother on that July afternoon, I was pale and thin; I had had another attack of fever before my departure. I told my brother to walk slowly as I couldn't keep up with him, although he had to lead the donkey, laden with my trunk.

When we got to the river the sun was high in the sky, and the only sound was the cicadas' shrilling among the olive trees. Nature was on fire and the sand in the river bed burned my bare feet, but we still had the steep road up to the village to climb, and I was exhausted. I asked my brother to let me rest a little. We sat down for a while in the shade of a lentisk bush. When I was rested we set off again. I think that I rode on the donkey for a short way, but it was uncomfortable and I soon dismounted.

We reached the village at nightfall. My mother welcomed me with a pitcher of curdled milk from her goats; this refreshing cool drink soon revived me.

As soon as we were alone, I explained to my mother that I had come home for good as the school was closed down and all the girls sent back to their families. She replied, '*Mektoub*. God's will be done. As long as I am alive, you will be protected, and after me God will have pity on you, just as he cares for the birds.'

From that day I tried to rid myself of the veneer of civilisation that I had acquired and not even think about it. Since the *Roumis* had rejected us, I resolved to become a Kabyle again.

I told my mother she must show me how to do all her work about the house, so that I could help her. The day after my return I started accompanying her to the well, with a pitcher on my back to fetch the water for our use. Then I went out to the shed and cleaned the animals' stalls as best I could.

In the spring, my mother, in common with all the village women, had started making potteryware for use in the house. She had walked a long way to find the right clay. During the Easter holidays I had watched her moistening and kneading the clay, picking out all the tiny pebbles to make the paste 'smooth as silk', to use her words. That year she had made a great number of usual objects: pitchers, amphoras, cooking pots, big dishes to cook *galettes* in, tall jars to hold water, oil and provisions of all sorts like dried vegetables and flour, as we had to stock up during the summer for the whole winter.

One morning she said, 'Today we are going to fire the pottery.'

My brothers set off first and dug a big hole in a field where the reaping had been done, then they came to fetch the objects, which they carried carefully one at a time. My mother joined them and I followed, carrying a few bowls in my arms. My mother and brothers had already collected a heap of rotten branches which would catch easily, like tinder.

The hole was filled with pottery, the biggest pieces at the bottom, then the medium sized, and finally the smallest ones. The whole lot was covered with earth and then the fire was lit and left to burn the whole day. At dusk, the fire was extinguished and we all carried the fired pottery back home. It was late by the time the work was finished, but everything had been put away before we sat down to eat the *couscous* with haricot beans and peas that mother had prepared.

Another day, the animals' shed had to be cleaned out and mother carried the manure in a wicker basket out to the field near the village. Then we started to prepare the fleece sheared from our sheep and lambs; mother left the wool to soak overnight in a mixture of ash and water before taking it next morning to wash in the stream.

The house we lived in, and which several generations had inhabited before us, was fairly large, made of stone and clay, probably. A roof was first made from reeds tied together with string woven from alfalfa grass and then covered with small tiles. This roof was supported by whole tree-trunks and the whole construction was further strengthened by two huge beams which went from one wall to the other.

Openings had been left under the roof in all the walls except the one facing the road; these were from twenty to forty centimetres square.

The house consisted of three parts of unequal size: the biggest was our living quarters. The floor was covered with a thick layer of fat lime, rubbed smooth with stones; women had rubbed away at this floor for days on end, removing every wrinkle, until it shone like a mirror and you could see your face in it. There were shelves along two walls, at waist height, and on these the amphoras filled with provisions were placed. Underneath these shelves, little alcoves had been hollowed out, in one of which water jars were stored; the others were used to shelter baby lambs and kids. The walls were smoothed with stones, the same as the floor.

Every spring mother went to collect a sort of bluish-white earth called *thoumlit* and gave the house a thorough spring-clean with a big besom made from a bundle of flexible broom-twigs; then she whitewashed the walls and even the roof. She even drew designs on the walls to make her house still more attractive.

The second part of the house was smaller, only about one metre high, made of stones and clay with a roof of branches covered with tamped down earth. Above it, on the side nearest the street wall, stood two square brick jars, rising nearly up to the roof: these were the *ikhoufanes*, essential to every house.

Next to the door there was just room for a bed, in case anyone wanted to rest there.

Three alcoves had been made in this little lean-to, to store fodder for the animals – two for the oxen and the other one for the donkey, all of which were kept in the cow-shed.

The third part of the house was the cattle-shed itself for the oxen, the donkey, the goats or the sheep. Under the roof of this part there was a sort of loft, the same size as the shed; this was used to store provisions or to accommodate one of the children, if he got married.

In the same courtyard, through the same gate, there were three other houses identical to ours, belonging to my brothers' relations. Higher up lived the old woman who always used to say to me, 'May God make the sun to shine out for you from behind the clouds.'

This was the restricted space in which I was now to live. I did not want to think of my past life any more, since I had to forget that I had been educated. I was determined to do my best about this. I was not unhappy, and what is more, I did not go hungry: I had my share of all the food there was.

The reaping was finished; a whole corner of the living-room was filled with a mixture of barley and corn. Mother said to me, 'Fadhma, my daughter, we are going to measure out our crop; we shall fill the *khoufi* with our own share and give the rest to the *sheikh* and to the poor.

She filled a ten-litre measure, poured out nine litres into the *khoufi* and put the tenth part on one side, continuing in this way until the heap was exhausted. Then she covered the *khoufi* with a large terracotta dish and sealed it up with clay, as the *khoufi* had four round holes in it big enough to put in an arm and take out the grain when required. These holes were closed with corks of the same size.

Out of God's tithe, mother set aside that which would go to the *sheikh* for feeding the destitute; she kept the rest to give to any paupers who turned up at the house.

The days passed, each one the same as the last. Mother combed and carded the wool; she taught me to spin so that she could weave me a blanket for the winter.

The figs and grapes began to ripen. Then all the village elders met for what was known as the *Dâoua*. No one living in the village was permitted to pick figs or grapes before the *Dâoua* had risen and the elders had given the word.

This delay of about two weeks was to allow the figs to ripen in sufficient quantities for all the villagers to benefit by them.

There would be a curse on anyone who defied this *Dâoua* and he would fall ill before the end of the fig season! No child would dare to pick a fig before permission was given, as they were all afraid of the village curse.

The village crier usually announced the raising of the ban from the top of the mosque, on 15 August. What excitement the next day! From first thing in the morning men and women alike, as well as all the children, were busy carrying home heavy baskets filled with black and white figs with the dew still fresh on them, figs the like of which I've never seen since!

We had a field of fig trees, known as *Thoujal*, where I loved going with mother as it was not too far from the village, but the way down was very steep and it was a stiff climb coming back. Some of the trees in this field must have been over a hundred years old; they were enormous, and when you stood under them you couldn't see the sun; the branches had to be supported to prevent them dragging on the ground and to let you pass beneath them. These figs were black on the outside and red inside and they were extremely sweet!

My mother used to say, 'Eat! eat!'

Every fig tree had its own name: one was called 'partridge-neck', another 'pomegranate' and one with very small fruit was known as 'the acorn-fig'.

The grapes, too, were magnificent: they hung down in huge bunches from the vines which clung to the poplars along the banks of the stream, reminding me of Taddert-ou-Fella. I used to climb up, hidden beneath the vines, to where the stream had its source, with the heavy red bunches nearly touching my head. We also had our vegetable patch beside the stream; long tender green beans trailed in the furrows where the water overflowed.

When the figs were ripe we carefully picked them one by one and spread them out to dry on reed trays. Mother and I went down to *Thoujal* every day until all the figs had been picked. When the trays were almost dry we placed them one on top of the other in a pile and at night we covered them over with slabs of cork to keep the dew off.

As soon as they were quite dry we brought them into the house and stored them in the corner where the grain had been kept.

Then we had to think about the grape harvest. We went to another field, called *Taferant* (the vineyard).

There were fine bunches of golden grapes, but they were not all to be eaten; we had to sell some to buy grain as our own crop was not sufficient to last the whole year. My brothers gathered the grapes and mother and I picked off any rotten fruit or any that the birds or wasps had got at. Then we filled up the *échouaris*, long wicker baskets joined together with a sort of bridge to fit on the back of a donkey or mule, with the panniers hanging down on each side. When a *chouari* was full we stopped picking and returned to the village and mother prepared supper. The evening before market day she would make a big *galette*, for whichever of my brothers to take with him when he went to Aumale to sell the grapes and bring back the load of grain, barley or corn. Mother gave him a little money; he put his *galette* in his saddle-bag with a few bunches of grapes and set off at dawn the next morning with the other villagers who had also to buy grain, like us.

If my brother had any black grapes left over, that he hadn't been able to sell for eating, he took them to the Moutier Mill. The owner of this press, which was known locally as the *Mouli*, bought these grapes cheaply to make wine.

August was over and we were well into September; we had had the first thunderstorms and ploughing the fields for turnips had begun. All the best figs had been brought inside; there were a few that were still soft and had to be eaten first. My brothers had sold all the grapes in the towns; sometimes they brought back enormous blood-red water-melons.

Although I was not unhappy with my mother and brothers, I was anxious about the future and when mother saw me looking worried she would say, '*Khoulef lomour i bhabhim.*' (Abandon yourself to the will of the Lord.)

Then it was October. We had sold the oxen that had been fattened up and only our small animals were left. The *sheikh* had been to perform the sacrifice for the ploughing. The village had bought the fattest oxen available to be slaughtered and distributed among all the inhabitants, who had to pay for their share. The animals intended for the sacrifice were first driven all round the houses so that the spirit of the harvest should be propitious and send abundant rains and we could expect a good crop of heavy ears of grain.

The day of the sacrifice we went to the well early and filled all the water jars and pitchers up to the brim; mother said we would need plenty of water to wash the meat as it would have been handled by so many people during the sharing-out. The *sheikh* blessed the animals (custom demanded that it should be a *sheikh* who had come from a distance for this ceremony, not one of the *marabouts* (holy men) from the village), which were then slaughtered and cut up; the hides and heads were sold, the meat divided into quarters and everyone received a generous share.

We had put the cooking-pots over the fire to boil very early and cleaned the vegetables; we had brought back a huge armful of tender thistles from the allotment and mother had rolled out a good quantity of *couscous*. We put our meat on to cook and sat in the doorway telling stories until the meat was ready. Mother did her spinning and I kept the fire going.

Still more days went by; the sowing had been done and my brothers went away for a few days. Mother and I were alone by the fireside as it was November and the nights were already cool. Our only light came from a smoking lamp hung on a post, against the wall above the fire. Then mother said, 'Fadhma, my daughter, there are certain things you ought to know.'

She told me all the things I have recounted at the beginning of this story. She told me everything she had suffered, all the martyrdom she had undergone because of Kaci, her evil brother.

'May God make him die without male heirs,' she said, 'so that all his property goes to his brothers.'

She also told me that the day she lost her case against my father, despairing of ever getting him to acknowledge me, she had tried to drown me in a pool of icy water, adding that she had pulled me out quickly, dried me and warmed me against her breast. The magistrate's wife, who was childless, had wanted to adopt me but mother preferred to keep me with her.

She told me about the episode of the prickly pears: how a wicked boy had thrown me into the hedge and she had spent all day picking the thorns out of my whole body. I also learned how she had taken me to the nuns to protect me from the other children's bullying, and how the nuns themselves had flogged me, so she had taken me away from them! Little by little as she talked, the heavy curtain before my eyes was rent and I began to understand many things that had previously been obscure.

I understood why I had been a pariah, why I was the only girl in the village to have been sent to the Christians. I understood all the sly allusions and why, at every quarrel, the insulting, hurtful word was flung in my face!

I recalled an episode from my schooldays: we were out for a walk, on the hillside near the abandoned house, when some travelling musicians passed us, on their way back from playing the tambourine in the village. One of them caught sight of me and pointed me out to one of the big girls, whispering something to her. I didn't know him, but he was giving away the secret of my birth! From that day, all the girls were in the know and whenever I tried to stand up for myself I always had the insulting word flung back at me.

In the village also certain women would look at me pityingly and I would overhear them saying, 'May God's curse be upon Kaci; it's his fault that such a pretty child is destined to be an outcast!'

Gradually, as my mother talked to me, I understood why I was different from the others; although I was the prettiest girl in the village no young man dared come to ask for my hand in marriage and so brave public opinion. I bore an indelible mark engraved on my forehead.

My mother spoke for a long time. She told me how much she had suffered when her brothers-in-law had tried to drive her out of her house and take all her property and her children.

'But,' she added, 'my sons have grown big now, they are men and the tattooing on my chin is worth more than a man's beard.'

She wept as she told me of her separation from her own family and of how she used to go to meet her mother beside the stream at Tagragra; she sobbed as she told me of her mother's death and how she had not been allowed to see her again, even as she lay dead, and of the burning sorrow that she still felt after so many years. I crept nearer to her, cradling her head in my arms and said, 'God has protected us till this day and will not abandon us.'

We went to bed. As I lay with closed eyes I re-lived my past life that had been so unhappy and filled with so many humiliations. I now understood the reason for this and why the other girls at school used to call me 'the Commissioner's daughter' because my mother had put me in the care of M. Demonque, the Administrator.

My brothers came back from their travels. Like many people in the village they had been off peddling cheap goods such as incense, antimony, little necklaces. These did not take up much room and could be carried on their backs in a small leather bag. They exchanged their merchandise for wool, or, in the plain where cereals were abundant, corn, barley or sorghum. They had made several excursions and brought back several loads on the donkey. Mother told me that we now had plenty of grain for the coming winter.

The olive crop was gathered in. As we passed a side track on the way to our olive grove mother told me that that was the spot where a certain man had been murdered. 'Every year,' she said, 'at the exact moment when he was killed, his last scream can be heard here. People call that the *aneza*.'

As soon as I approached that place I instinctively walked faster for fear of hearing the *aneza*. Our field was enormous, with hundreds and hundreds of olive trees, but the soil was shaly and not really suitable for olives and they only bore fruit every second year.

Nevertheless we had sufficient stocks of oil to last the year.

My brothers also beat the oak trees so that we could collect the acorns which were as big as walnuts and very sweet; the corner of the room where we stored the crops was filled up with piles of acorns. My mother lit a huge log fire which she kept burning fiercely all day – from dawn to nightfall. She spread the acorns out on big dishes and put them on the fire to dry so that they wouldn't get worm-eaten. As soon as one dish began to roast she grabbed it with a cloth and emptied it on to the racks placed on the beams above the fireplace, so that the acorns would finish drying by spring.

Winter came but we did not feel the cold. We kept the fire burning night and day with the huge logs that had been chopped during the summer, to which we added oil-cakes. We only went out to fetch water from the well.

One Friday, the day for prayer in my mother's religion, she stayed at home while I went to the well with the other girls. I remember that on the way back my hands were so frozen that I could scarcely hold on to the pitcher of water that I was carrying on my back. When I got home, mother had just finished her ablutions; she took the pitcher from me, put it down and plunged my hands into the warm water. That did me good. Then she gave me a bowl of warm milk from the goats she had just milked. The last few days our ewes and goats had given birth to baby lambs and kids. Then I sat down by the fire on a stool made out of a large log. The snow continued to fall all that day and the whole night: snowflakes like fleece reminded me of the snow that fell in Taddert-ou-Fella. I imagined I could hear the torrent roaring as its waters rushed down into the 'bathing-pool' and gushed out again with the current; I could see in my mind's eye its enchanted banks covered with buttercups and violets; the icy slopes we used to slide down below the abandoned house; the snowballs – everything that represented my childhood. I heaved a deep sigh, thinking, 'Never again!'

I realised that my mother was gazing at me anxiously.

'What are you thinking about now?'

'Nothing . . . '

We had to stay at home the whole of the next day. We put out utensils to collect the water that dripped from the roof. Only my brothers ventured out to collect olive branches for the animals.

My old friend Yemma Tassâdit came to get warm by our fire and, seeing the snow falling and the wind blowing she said, as she watched me sifting the grain to be ground for the evening meal, '*Dhamerdhil*, it's the day borrowed for the goat,' and as I looked at her in bewilderment she said, 'What! You don't know that story?

'In the olden times, long long ago,' she began, 'when the good Lord listened to the miseries of the world, there lived a very old woman, whose only possession was a goat, which kept her company and gave her milk.

'The old woman and the goat lived side by side in a tumbledown hut outside the village. Every day the old woman went out with her companion; the one ate the green shoots, the other collected bundles of firewood and picked edible herbs for her meals. Every evening the two of them returned to their hut where they spent the night and the next day they began the same routine.

'But one year the month of January was very severe. For thirty days and thirty nights it never stopped raining or snowing and all this time the old woman and her goat had to stay shut in.

'When January was over, the first day of February was gloriously fine: the sky was blue and the bright sun seemed a harbinger of spring. The old woman and her goat could leave their refuge at last and go out once more into the fields. However, the old woman looked up into the sky and spat at the month that was just over.

'They spent the whole day in the forest, the goat eating the tender shoots, the old woman collecting a huge bundle of firewood and looking for the little green herbs that were just showing through the snow.

But when they were about to return home a blustering wind began to blow, the sky grew dark and heavy black clouds were rent with huge raindrops. In an instant the stream they had crossed that morning had become a tumultuous muddy torrent and when they tried to wade across they were carried away by the current; several days passed before their bodies were found washed up on the bank of the river.

'January had been so insulted when the old woman spat at him that he had gone in search of February, his successor, and asked him to lend him a day, so that the old woman could be punished. February agreed to the request and since then, the return of wintry weather is known as "the day borrowed for the goat".'

My old friend finished telling her story and I had finished sifting my grain; she went back to her children's house and I settled down to my grinding. I would turn first with one hand and then with the other, as each arm got tired, and all the time I kept pouring handfuls of grain into the hole at the top of the mill; the flour gradually accumulated in a little receptacle hollowed out of the clay. As I ground I sometimes sang the songs of the mill and dreamed of my past life when I was home on holiday and when my eyes were sore in the evening I would rest my head on my mother's lap while she was grinding her grain. For many years I had suffered from my eyes and had to go to the Christian mission to have drops put in and one of the Brothers would say to me, '*Ldi titim*, open your eye!'

I no longer had trouble with my eyes now; I was nearly grown-up, but my future seemed very black.

My brothers just then arrived back from the *tajmâat* (meeting-place), walking through the snow, perched on *kabkabs* (stilts). Lamine had bought some sheep and they said they were going to slaughter them in honour of the snow, to propitiate it so that we should have a good year with abundant crops.

Mother had to cook *galettes* for our midday meal; she gave us each a good helping then filled a basket with figs from the provision jar and placed a bowl of whey in front of each of us. When all four of us had eaten as much as we wanted we set about our several tasks. My brothers wove alfalfa grass into ropes; my mother took up her distaff and I went on with my spinning. We all sat round the fire, pushing a handful of oil-cakes on to it from time to time.

That evening the sheep were slaughtered and everyone in the village had their share of the meat, so that everybody could have a good meal in honour of the snow.

The next day the sun shone again, the snow melted and we could go to fetch water from the well.

I had heard that the White Sisters who had been in Tagmount since 1894, took in a few boarders. I had got someone who knew the Mother Superior to inquire if she would be prepared to accept me in return for some work. She sent back a reply in the negative and I didn't give the matter any further thought.

The Administrator summoned me, and my brother went with me to see what it was about. When we arrived the cook received me and went to tell his master I was there and show him the summons. He came back with a voucher authorising me to collect the sum of thirty francs from the paymaster. So that was why the Administrator had made me come all the way from my village and hire a mule, just for thirty francs! Since I was there, I collected the money and returned to my village.

One morning in February my mother said to me, 'You and I are going to see the *sheikh*; he is very sensible and will advise me what to do, as I've received an offer of marrige for you, but the match doesn't suit me: the family is tainted. So I'm going to consult the *sheikh* and his wife, Lalla Yamina.'

We set off on foot as it wasn't far, leaving my brothers to look after the house and the animals.

The sky was blue, the weather mild, the birds were singing in the bushes; the trees were in bud and we could feel that spring was on the way, although few flowers were out yet, except for some violets on the bank of the river. It was about noon when we arrived at the *sheikh*'s village. He lived alone with his family in a big house surrounded by fig trees and cactus hedges.

We were made welcome by the *sheikh*'s wife, a woman in her fifties; mother gave her the offering we had brought and promised her a live sheep if my future were properly assured. Lalla Yamina had a brown face with big, black, intelligent eyes; she was a good friend to my mother and for many years she had been a great help to her, and always of good counsel.

Mother and I followed our hostess into a large room that was used for prayers and to receive guests. We spent the whole day and the night there.

The next morning, immediately after the dawn prayer, Lalla Yamina said to mother, 'You must return home as something has happened, but don't worry about your daughter, she will be happy and soon there will be no need for you to fear for her future. Last night, while I was thinking about her, I had a dream which went like this: I was holding a fine piece of meat in my hands, but it began to smell bad; I washed it and covered it with salt and spices and gave it to you.'

She gave my mother several kilos of semolina and some dried meat and we set off back home.

When we got back it was nearly nine o'clock but the house was shut up and the animals had not been let out.

Mother realised that something was wrong. She ran to the house where the young men of the *Akham guelmezien* district slept. She found it shut up as they had all left for work, except for one youngster who told her, 'Your son Lâmara left this morning for the city with one of his friends. They are going to Souk-Arhas, he must have got to Tizi-Ouzou to catch the train.'

Today, half a century later, I can still see the despair on my mother's face! When she returned she was unrecognisable: heavy sobs shook her breast and huge tears fell from her eyes. She wanted to leave for Tizi-Ouzou to bring her son back but I told her it would be too late by the time she got there . . .

For days and days on end she refused to eat. Nothing I could say would console her; I assured her she was not alone, she still had me as well as my eldest brother, but she replied with the proverb, 'When the heart and liver are missing, what use are the lungs?'

I realised that for my mother, only my brother Lâmara counted; at least that was what I believed at the time. Her youngest son had always been her favourite, as he was very handsome: he had a long face, light complexion, a straight nose, smiling mouth and big blue-green eyes, like my mother's. She admitted to me later that whenever she had to share anything out, she couldn't help giving him the best portion. That had given rise to many scenes as my elder brother was jealous of the younger one.

When we opened up the house I went straight to the trunk where I had put away the money my mother had entrusted to me, after the sale of the oxen. Half the money had gone, my brother must have taken it for his travelling expenses. Mother wept for a long time, but gradually she resumed her daily work. It was the weeding season and every day we were up at dawn and as soon as we had fetched water for the mosque and our own use, we went off to the fields. We loosened the soil in every row with a very small hoe and pulled out all the weeds. We took food to eat for midday and mid-afternoon (*galette* and dried figs). We returned home to eat in the evening, tired but happy from these fine days in the open air.

February was over and we were into March when, one morning, I saw the Mother Superior of Tagmount arriving. She told me that she had submitted my application to the Mother General, who wanted to see me.

I wasn't sure at first if I should go with her, but then I got dressed and left with her . . . I was taken to a tall, dark nun with a rather severe expression who told me to go to the Hospital at Aïth-Manegueleth, saying she had sent me, and to ask for Mother Saint-Matthew. But before that she asked me if we had been taught anything about religion at school. I told her, no, not a word, as it was a lay school and supposed to be non-sectarian. She handed me two francs for the hire of a mule and the audience was over.

When I came home and talked to mother she began to weep.

'You are going to leave me, too . . . First your brother and now you. I had got used to having you at home; you kept me company and I could rely on you to look after the house.'

It took me a few days to make up my mind, and then I decided to go.

So I left my village after seven months. I had been happy with my mother and brothers. I had had a home, I was no longer the pariah I had always been; but I realised that this existence could not last: my mother was my sole protector and she could die and I would be alone.

I left one Thursday morning. March had brought warmer weather, the sky was clear, the birds sang and the buds were beginning to burst on the trees where tiny leaves were already visible. The ploughed fields were bright green; nature was celebrating the new season of the year. The water in the river bubbled over the pebbles, and violets and buttercups were out on either bank. The oleanders were in bud and the olive trees in flower.

Perched on my mule behind my trunk, I feasted my eyes on this scene which I was not to view again for a very long time, and then for very short periods. In fact, after 1898, I only saw my village again three times, at long intervals, never again taking the route by which I was then leaving.

I took the road that sloped down to the river, but then it was uphill again to Aït-Yenni, downhill again, across the Djemâa River and up the hill to Aïth-Manegueleth. But this time I did not have to travel on foot as I had always done in my childhood.

Mother had wept bitterly when she saw me off. 'If ever you need anything,' she said, 'or if you are unhappy, remember that as long as I live my home is yours.'

I wept as well, but I had said to myself, 'I must leave! I must be on my way again! Such has been my lot since my birth, never have I had a place I could call my home!'

We went a very long way round as my brother wasn't sure where the hospital was. We only arrived at our destination at noon.

The Hospital at Aïth-Manegueleth

From the first moment when I stood before the frontage of the hospital I recognised my dream: the same colonnades that I had seen when the gigantic bird picked me up from the bottom of the ravine, where I was lying between walls of ice, and deposited me on a little plateau where there stood a building that I had never seen before.

I immediately thought, 'There is no doubt that this is where my destiny will be fulfilled.'

The frontage of the hospital was about five hundred feet wide. The colonnades bordered a sort of gallery which we called 'the corridor'. From the outside, you went through a large gate and then up a few steps into the gallery. Then you went into a long passage with doors on each side leading to the parlour, the dispensary, the women's and men's wards, the linen-room and kitchen. At the end there was a door to the outside.

The day I arrived, I entered by 'the corridor' where I found the janitor, a gnome-like creature.

He went to fetch a nun who took me to Mother Saint-Matthew. I remember my surprise at finding myself in the presence of a young woman of pleasant appearance as the name Matthew had for some reason made me expect someone old and shrivelled up.

Mother Saint-Matthew told me that she had been warned to expect me by the Mother General, Mother Salome. I would be fed, all my expenses paid and, in addition, would earn ten francs a month. I accepted and went back to let my brother know of the arrangements before he returned home. Then I followed the nun who was to take me in hand. I went with her to a room on a lower level on the other side of the main building.

There I found creatures of all ages; with few exceptions they had all been patients in the hospital and still had scars and sores visible on their bodies. When I was asked what my name was, and replied 'Marguerite', I was told that I had no right to a Christian name as I hadn't been baptised, and so I became 'Fadhma from Tagmount'. That already put a damper on my spirits.

My life was now to be spent among these creatures: not one of them knew a word of French, not one had been to school. I sat down to eat with them. At that time there was an outbuilding behind the kitchen that was used as our refectory. In the evening I was shown where I was to sleep – a straw mattress on trestles, with all the other women in their dormitory. Next to it was a room which was a work-room during the day; a bed was made up there for the nun who was in charge of us.

The next morning we got up at five, we washed and dressed and at six the bell rang for mass. All these girls and women went up to the chapel with our nun in charge. We went along the gallery, up a staircase to a long passage which led to the nuns' dormitory, their reading-room and the chapel. It opened out onto a balcony which ran the whole length of the colonnaded gallery down below.

As I didn't understand anything of the mass I didn't want to attend and remained sitting in the passage until it was over. A White Father had come to say mass for the nuns, as on every morning. At the end of the service, when I heard them singing a hymn, I suddenly emerged from my daydream: I had heard this hymn before. Then I was suddenly back in Taddert-ou-Fella, and I recalled our walks by moonlight in the month of May when we used to go to hear the congregation singing.

When mass was over, the girls filed out of the chapel after the nuns. We had our breakfast and then went about our respective duties. I was presented to the Father Superior who had said mass. He asked me a lot of questions that I can't remember any more, as I was busy taking in his appearance. He seemed to me to be quite regal in his bearing, with his white beard reaching down to his chest, his long face with the aquiline nose and deep-set, blue eyes. He was in the habit of raising one finger as he spoke and imperceptibly winking one eye; he gave the impression of weighing every word before he uttered it. When I rejoined my companions, I was sent to work in the linen-room with Sister Chantal.

On the way I had gone past the women's ward and seen all the diseases and ailments: I was particularly struck by the number of sores – many on the face. I noticed one woman whose face was one huge ulcer, covered with ointment and dressings.

I still have a confused and painful impression of that period of my life. Everyone kept talking about God, everything had to be done for the love of God, but you felt you were being spied upon, everything you said was judged and reported to the Mother Superior. I thought I was going to be back in the friendly atmosphere of Taddert-ou-Fella but I was disappointed and baffled. When I mentioned that there was some good to be found in all religions, it was considered blasphemous.

The prayers had been translated into Kabyle: the *Ave Maria*, 'Our Father', the *Credo*, and the nuns pegged away at drumming these expressions into our rebellious heads. And I couldn't help smiling when I heard the nuns' way of pronouncing the Kabyle language.

Day after day went by and by dint of continuous effort, I gradually began to get used to this life.

Among these girls there were some who were married; I had noticed one whose face seemed vaguely familiar. Her name was Félicité, but I overheard someone refer to her in Kabyle as Tassâdit-Aïth-Ouchen, and I recognised her as one of the 'big girls' who had lived at the convent at Ouadhias. When she saw me she whispered something to her neighbour . . . Her husband had been a cook for the Fathers at Aïth-Yenni and had come back to the hospital with tuberculosis and she had come with him. There was another very young woman from Ouadhias whose husband was the hospital baker. Both of them were expecting babies and the nuns showed particular concern for them. They lived apart from the rest of us, with their own husbands, one at the bakery, the other in a room behind the ironing-room, but both of them worked with us.

There was also an Arab girl from the Atafs, named Josephine, with a rodent ulcer that had eaten away her whole nose, leaving only the nostrils. She dressed in European fashion and was the only one who spoke French. Another married woman, who lived in the village, came to earn a few pence helping with sewing or washing. Still another one boarded with us, but her husband lived in Kerrata; she was expecting a baby also; she wanted to return to her own region as soon as her husband could come and fetch her. But the nicest of all these was Fadhma-t-Yehyalen, who came from the village of Taourirth – my mother's birthplace. She was very ill and had sores from scurvy all over her neck. But what a sweet nature she had! Her faith was very strong: she was a real little saint who later became a nun in the Order of the Good Shepherd.

The hardest thing about the hospital was the way the sick and the healthy had to live cheek by jowl. The nuns didn't hesitate to send us to nurse a tuberculous woman, without any regard for the danger of infection to which we were exposed. One girl had developed the disease after working all day in the laundry, through the winter, and never getting properly dry. At least, that's what she said; this poor girl's eyes were permanently gummed up and encrusted. They called her L'Djohar-n-Sidi-Ali-ou-Moussa, as her parents came from the village of that name. When I arrived she was already too ill to get up but the other girls went to sit with her every day as she remained very cheerful. One of the Fathers – an excellent man – paid out of his own pocket for her to enjoy some of her favourite dishes; for example, he had had a *couscous* with chicken made for her, knowing that she wasn't going to recover. I went to see her myself, although I have always shrunk from the sight of physical suffering.

Eventually, I started going to chapel and attending mass; I liked to hear the hymns; some of the nuns had very beautiful voices, and I've always responded to the charm of music.

Easter was approaching. During Holy Week we went to the service at the monastery every day. There was now a whole flock of us: Mother Denise had sent a batch of girls from Tagmount that I had known when they were beggars; many others had been discharged from the ward, more or less cured – some of them still had inflamed, ulcerated eyelids. We now had a uniform: white cretonne *gandouras* for Sundays and holidays, brown cretonne for every day, with sack-cloth aprons and cotton headscarves.

I liked these Holy Week services because of the liturgical chants and the organ music. As for the Catholic religion, I don't think I was ever truly convinced. But I believe sincerely in God.

When the Fathers declared that only those who had been baptised would go to heaven, I didn't believe them. I thought of my mother, of all that she had suffered, the three months a year she spent fasting (for besides Ramadan, she imposed supplementary fasts on herself), of the heavy loads of water she took it upon herself to carry to the mosque in all weathers and I thought, 'Is it possible that my mother will not go to heaven?'

The Fathers lived about two kilometres from the hospital. To get to the monastery we walked along the main road, then turned off along a little path. That year it snowed throughout Holy Week and we had to make our way through the snow to the service, walking in a croco-dile, two by two. But Easter Sunday was fine and we enjoyed a long walk. The next day we resumed our daily routine: morning mass, breakfast, work and catechism for the women and girls.

The countryside around the hospital was rather like that around Taddert-ou-Fella: here, also we were surrounded by hills; the village of Ouarzen stood atop one of these and Taourirth on the other; the road ran along the whole north side of the building and to the east, on another hill, was Mme Pacquereau's house. She was a midwife who trained Kabyle women who came from the surrounding villages. She was very taciturn – she must have been through difficult times.

As the dormitory had become too small and the sinks for doing the washing were too far away, Father Baldit decided to build a laundry with a new dormitory over it. In spring he blessed the first stone and by the autumn we had moved in. As this dormitory was linked to the terrace by a balcony we could get to chapel without having to go downstairs; it was much more convenient and much nearer. A cubicle was screened off in the middle of the dormitory for the nun in charge.

Among the nuns there were many foreigners. Some of them spoke very bad French. I was particularly fond of one Dutch nun who was in charge of the women's ward; sometimes, on my way to the linen-room, I stopped to say hello to her, but this annoyed Sister Chantal who was middle-aged and rather aloof. She was the one who used to read us the life of Dom Bosco while we sat mending and darning the patients' none-too-clean bed-linen. During the two years that I spent at the hospital, I nearly always worked with her.

One day a patient in the men's ward died; he was a Christian, known as Tahar-de-la-salle. He had been ill for a long time, with tuberculosis, I think. Everyone was assembled in the chapel when I arrived and took my place. In this instance the boys from the mission school and the assistant teachers, employed by the Fathers, were also there. I didn't take particular notice of anyone, but someone had noticed me, I learned a few days later.

Father Baldit summoned me to the parlour. I wondered what I could possibly have said this time, as on several occasions I had been told off for having made fun of someone, or for making un-Christian remarks. But now it was something else. Father Baldit had received an offer of marriage for me and wanted to know what I thought. I had been there about three months. I replied that if he thought the young man would make a good husband I would not refuse him. Then I left. The suitor was one of the assistant teachers who came from Ighil-Ali, but at the time I didn't attach any importance to this detail.

I was different from the other girls and consequently felt the weight of their jealousy and the nuns' suspicion. Because I had been educated at the lay school I was thought to know a lot about life, whereas in fact I knew nothing, alas!

The holidays were over. One day Father Baldit told me that the marriage plan had fallen through as the young man's parents had refused their consent and the father had even threatened to kill him if he defied him. As I didn't know the young man, this news left me indifferent. The year had passed; my mother had come to see me once or twice; I gave her the little money I had earned, and two sheets that I had brought back from school, to console her. We were now sleeping in the new dormitory, on straw mattresses, on the bare ground. The number of girls had increased. Although I had not been baptised, Father Baldit used me to teach the others the catechism, as I was considered educated. On Sundays, he heard them recite what they had learned, but as soon as my back was turned, I felt that they were whispering about me.

What surprised me the most about the world I now found myself in, was the enormous prestige enjoyed by representatives of the male sex, even the most unprepossessing. Our janitor was a sort of hybrid creature, half man, half gorilla: his forehead was low and mulish, his eyes were continuously running with a supurating discharge, he had a squashed, broken nose, drooping lips and his big yellow teeth were rotten and irregular. Added to which he limped badly as one of his legs was stiff from rheumatism. He used to squat all day in the middle of the colonnaded gallery, opposite the stairs.

One morning as we were coming back from mass, the nun in charge of us said, 'You mustn't go through the gallery any more. You must leave the chapel by the door at the back.'

I looked up in surprise and asked, 'Why, Sister?'

'Because there are men there,' she replied.

'Men? But there's only the janitor.'

'Well, and isn't he a man?'

'No, Sister,' I retorted firmly.

'What is he then, a woman?'

'No, he isn't a woman, but he isn't a man. He's a creature apart.

He's the janitor, that's all.'

After that we never passed through the gallery on our way back from mass.

Christmas was approaching; we were preparing to celebrate it in fitting manner: we were learning carols and the nuns were practising the organ. At the hospital we sang what was known as 'The Royal Mass'. On Sunday evening we celebrated vespers and the Father who officiated brought back a memory which had long haunted me and which I had never been able to explain: it was of a place of darkness where bright light fell and where a person dressed in strange fashion moved slowly holding in his hands what seemed a kind of sun. For a long time at Taddert-ou-Fella I had puzzled over the meaning of this fairy-like picture . . . Now I suddenly understood: it went right back to the dark chapel at Ouadhias where I had been taken as a tiny child, and in this candle-lit chapel a priest, dressed in sacerdotal vestments, held the monstrance in his hands.

At the 1898 midnight mass the nuns sang glorious hymns (I can still hear Sister Emmanuel's powerful harmonious voice breaking into 'Christian Midnight'). After mass there was a Christmas supper: the nuns surpassed themselves and we had a real feast. And there was a surprise gift for everyone.

I had become very devout; I think that there was a certain amount of superstition in my piety: I hoped one day to hear the statues of the Virgin and the Sacred Heart speak to me and tell me what I must do. I made myself spend long periods before the stations of the cross, fervently praying to God and the Virgin Mary for help, begging them to open up a way for me out of the impasse in which I found myself.

Sometimes I seemed to hear a voice in my heart saying, as on the *Via dolorosa*, 'Patience, my child! Patience! Do not lose faith!' And I even thought seriously of becoming a nun, like these Sisters who had sacrificed their youth in the service of God and for those less fortunate than themselves. There were a number of conversions at that time. Mature men and women were becoming Christians. I think this was due to the great generosity of the Fathers at that period. All the people who worked at the hospital, including the janitor, wanted to abandon Islam. And on Sundays the chapel was full to suffocation.

I can still recall the snow that year which fell deeper even than at

Taddert-ou-Fella, as Michelet is at a higher altitude than Fort-National. I can still see the long, sharp icicles hanging like huge, heavy swords from the roof. Sister Chantal set up her sewing machine in the confined space of the linen-room, where we sat on benches placed against the lockers for the patients' linen. She put an old basin on the floor, filled with glowing embers, damped down with a thick layer of ash. Sometimes some poor girl would come in from the outside completely frozen through and would scrabble her fingers in the ash to warm them. If the Sister caught sight of her she would make her kiss the ground. This was the standard punishment inflicted on all the girls who disobeyed her: they had to kiss the ground before they returned to work.

The snow at the hospital has not left me with the same happy memories as at Taddert-ou-Fella. Here there were no games, no snowballs, no snowman, everything was cheerless, everything had to be done for God and offered to God, so this period of my life has left me with a taste of ashes.

Winter had slipped away. I had learned by chance that my former schoolfellow Mlle Larab (Inès) had been appointed to teach at the Aïth-Hichem primary school and that the Administrator Masselot had asked the nuns if they wanted to take over the Taddert-ou-Fella school, but they had refused the offer. Father Baldit had let me know that I couldn't be accepted as a novice, for family reasons.

I never made any attempt to write to Mme Sahuc, although I knew that she was now the head of the Miliana Normal College. I never asked her for any favours, any more than from M. Masselot. For all that I discovered that she had tried to do me harm, even from a distance: one day the Mother Superior summoned me to the parlour and read me what Mme Sahuc had said about me in the report she had drawn up on her pupils. My report was very bad. And in addition, she stated that as I came from a well-to-do family, I didn't need any help!

I asked Mother Saint-John if she would have accepted me if she had known this beforehand. She said, 'No!'

I had now been at the hospital for nearly a year. Saint Joseph's day had come and gone and soon it would be Easter, with services held at the monastery, but for some reason I felt sad and anxious.

One Sunday we had a pleasant surprise: we were given a delicious roast for dinner. We hadn't had a good meal like this for ages; there was even a sort of dessert. They told us it was roast rabbit, or possibly a baby kid. A few days later the mystery was cleared up, when some of the girls discovered the head and skin of Sister Purification's cat thrown into a hole: we had eaten cat and found it delicious!

In the spring some of the Ouadhias girls walked over to see us. They talked in a very nasty way about Germaine, one of my school-fellows from Taddert-ou-Fella; they mimicked the way she said, 'My name is Germaine, my teacher gave me this name . . . ' and then burst out laughing.

I didn't like anyone making fun of Mme Malaval, nor of her pupils and I retorted that they were quite as good as the girls from Ouadhias and that Germaine was quite right to say her teacher had given her that name. The nun in charge of us took the Ouadhias girls' part, so I wrote to my brother to come and fetch me home. I gave the letter to the Mother Superior who agreed to post it. But that evening Father Justrob sent for me and asked why I wanted to leave. I told him I had had enough. He reasoned with me kindly, advising me to be patient for a little longer: things would be settled sooner than I thought.

Father Baldit had given me a copy of *The Imitation of Jesus Christ* and I began to read this wonderful book.

One Sunday our nun told us we were going for an outing. We set off early in the morning and went to Aïth-Hichem, and I was able to see my old friend Inès again; she had lost a lot of weight, but she said she was happy. She now dressed in French fashion and I noticed on her bed one of our old *gandouras* which she was making into a skirt. She told me she still received *The Classroom Reader*, a magazine we used to read at school. She took a pile of these off a shelf, offering to lend them to me, but she reckoned without the nuns: the magazines were confiscated, I never managed to read them, as we were not allowed any secular amusement.

Summer came. The hospital was surrounded by a field of fig trees and the nuns had a beautiful garden with a marvellous spring, but we couldn't visit it unless we were escorted or when we were out walking in a crocodile. Some of my companions were nice; Alice for example was a very sweet girl and so was Seltana, the baker's wife. But I couldn't speak French with any of them and I was never alone with my friend Inès, so we could never talk about old times at Taddert-ou-Fella. There was always some third person present coming between us.

I had suffered a great sorrow: Sister Emmanuel, the nun I was so fond of, had fallen ill; for weeks on end she lay between life and death, then one day she was brought down to be taken to Saint-Charles. I went to see her in the parlour and wept bitterly as she had been so sweet and understanding to me, when my heart was so hungry for affection.

Days dragged by and I was at the end of my tether. I had asked the Mother Superior to find me work in France. She replied that she would see but I still felt I was surrounded by mistrust and jealousy.

Father Baldit had told me of one or two offers of marriage he had received on my behalf; they didn't seem to have much advantage to me and I turned them down.

One day Father Carisson came to tell me he had found me work at the Deputy Administrator's in Michelet.

'I'll never be anyone's servant,' I replied, 'especially in the Kabyle region,' and no more was said about the matter.

In the spring my mother had been to visit me. She had been to *Sheikh* Mohand's sanctuary and had met Mme Achab, a former pupil of my school, and now the teacher at the Azrou-ou-Quelal primary school. She bitterly reproached my mother for having put me with the nuns where there was the danger I would abandon Islam. Mother told me she was most upset by this storm of abuse. I replied that she and I were the best judges and it was nobody else's business.

While Sister Chantal and I were sewing in the linen-room, I caught her examining my face closely; this wasn't the first time I had noticed her doing this, as if she was searching for some half-forgotten memory.

'Why are you looking at me like that, Sister?' I asked. 'What's so peculiar about my face?'

'Fadhma,' she asked, 'were you ever with the White Sisters?'

'Yes, but I was very small and I can't remember anything about it.'

'That's what it is. I was there at the time.'

And she told me with a laugh how Sister Suzanne had treated me and recounted the scene in the corridor when Father Grandjacquet, who was then in charge of the convent, had seen me covered in excrement; she told me what a fuss my mother had made about what to her was a completely insignificant incident. She had often wondered what had become of me; my features had changed and she had only recognised me by my eyes.

Summer was drawing on. One Sunday as we were coming out of chapel after vespers, I was accosted by old Hemmama-t-Madour, who had converted to Christianity and seemed a sincere believer. She took me on one side and said, 'Belkacem has returned from Ighil-Ali to teach at the school here; he would like to know if you would agree to marry him, if he asked the Father Superior.'

I wasn't very sure of this woman so I gave her an evasive answer. I was working with Seltana whom I trusted. She was married and lived with her husband at the bakery and was free to come and go as she pleased. I told her what old Hemmama had said and she asked me if I knew how to write a letter.

'Yes,' I replied.

'Write a letter setting our your conditions and I'll see that the young man gets it, as he comes every day to the hospital, to keep the janitor company.'

I wrote my letter and advised my suitor – if he was sure he wanted to get married – to put his request directly to Father Baldit, rather than sending messages by old women.

I gave the note to Seltana who, under my very eyes, put it straight into the hands of the young man who was standing next to Négro.

In the evening of 15 August, the Feast of the Assumption, we were kneeling beside our beds and I was reciting the prayers while the other girls and women repeated the responses. Suddenly our nun tapped me on the shoulder.

'The Father Superior wants to see you in the parlour.'

I went downstairs, my heart beating fast. Father Baldit was walking up and down as usual. As soon as I entered he said, 'That young man who asked you to marry him last year has returned. He has fallen out with his family and wants you to be his wife. What must I tell him?'

'What do you advise me to do, Father? What do you know about this young man?'

He simply replied, 'He's very nice.'

And that was the only reference he was able to give me.

I accepted the offer and a day or two later the nuns organised a meeting in the parlour between me and my suitor.

I was very shy and blushed furiously; he seemed very young to me, but he tried to hide his feelings.

And that's how my marriage was decided on 15 August 1899.

I did not know my future husband; he did not know me either; we were not from the same tribe; his village was on the other side of the mountain, in Little Kabylia. In a word, everything seemed to separate us, but by the will of God my destiny and his were to be united.

When I think of this period I am astounded at our carefree attitude and I wonder how we managed to make out. I was sixteen, the young man was eighteen, we had no home, no money, all we possessed was our youth and hope. And the good Lord did the rest: a veritable miracle.

The bird in my dream had deposited me in front of the hospital colonnades; and there in fact my destiny was realised.

When I came back to the dormitory the women and girls were in bed already. They only heard the news a few days later when the nuns provided a little trousseau for me and Tassâdit (later christened Blanche) who were to be married the same day, 24 August. They gave us two or three *gandouras*, including one white one for our baptism and the wedding ceremony, six cotton chemises, six towels, one silk headscarf and two of cotton, and a red woollen sash like the soldiers used to wear.

Old Hammama-t-Madour found us a room in Ouarzen for a few months, and that's where we lived until 1 November 1899.

II

I Become Part
of the Amrouche Family

My Marriage

The evening before my wedding, Chlili and Merzoug, two of my fiancé's friends, arrived from Ighil-Ali with his cousin, El Madani-ou-Amrouche. They all slept over at the monastery. The next day my brother Lâmara arrived as soon as it was light, bringing a message from my mother who was unwell; a young Christian school-friend of my future husband was there to act as best man.

I haven't a very clear recollection of how things went that morning. I know that we all set off before breakfast as usual, dressed in our white *gandourahs*, to walk two by two to the monastery where the baptism and the wedding were to take place. Sister Chantal had agreed to act as my godmother. Blanche and I were then baptised in the name of the Father, the Son and the Holy Ghost.

The marriage was performed by Father Ben Mira, one of the two Arabs among the White Fathers, who had been converted by Cardinal Lavigerie.

Blanche and I returned to the hospital with our companions. On the way back I was stopped by my brother who demanded the customary dowry – the sum which the fiancé is supposed to give his bride's family, to be returned in case of divorce. In my case, my husband had not had his family's consent to the match, so the missionaries had agreed to provide the dowry. I went to find Mother Saint-John who gave me the money and Lâmara left, not completely satisfied as he reckoned I was worth more! He returned to our village the same evening, with his companion.

Later that evening someone from the village came to fetch Blanche and me to take us to the feast of *couscous* and mutton that my husband had ordered for all the guests and that had been cooked by the Akhli-Aïth-El-Houcine family. Cousin Madani wasn't sure whether Blanche or I was Belkacem's wife and kept inquiring anxiously, 'Which one is it? Which is the one?' (I have to admit that Blanche was not a beauty!)

Dishes of *couscous* and meat were put aside for the Fathers and the nuns. Then the guests all helped themselves from one enormous wooden bowl of *couscous*. I can't remember whether I managed to eat a little. Then we went to Akhli's house where games were organised for the men and we didn't get to bed till far into the night. From that day I never felt alone again. From now on, there were two of us, for better or for worse.

The next day I returned to the hospital. Mother Saint-John gave me a rush mat and lent me four woollen blankets and two sheets. I still had a few things that I had brought in my trunk from Taddert-ou-Fella, besides the little trousseau the nuns had given me. My husband borrowed a donkey and we loaded everything on to its back. I said goodbye to Malha, to Sister John of God – a sweet little nun who I called 'Little Sister Dolly'; I went to pay my respects to Sister Chantal and Mother Saint-John and left to begin my new life.

The disposition of the house at Ouarzen, found for us by old Hemmama, was more or less the same as my mother's. But there the similarity ended: this house was empty, whereas my mother's was full up, neat and clean with the earth floor and the walls all whitened and lovingly maintained.

I put the mat and blankets down in one corner, on the raised platform intended for the men; they would only be unrolled in the evening. The hospital carter Touderth had his house in the same courtyard with his mother, his wife and two daughters.

I think it was on the Friday after my wedding that I first saw Hemma, my husband's maternal uncle, arrive. He came on Thursday evening, slept and ate with us, went off to sell his wool at the Friday market, to be back home on Saturday morning. The day after his arrival he told his nephew, Belkacem, that he intended to take us back with him to Ighil-Ali, to introduce me to the family. He could assure us that my husband need have nothing to fear from his father as I was a good-looking girl.

So we left on Saturday 26 August, calling first at the hospital. I asked the Mother Superior for the small sum of money still owing to me – about thirty francs I think. It was very hot. We did not get to Ighil-Ali till evening.

My first impression on entering my parents-in-law's home was surprise. The heavy gates of the carriage entrance – gates that defied the centuries – swung open to reveal a vast courtyard, enclosed on all sides by high walls, but it was very light that summer's day.

I alighted from my mule, my mother-in-law kissed me on the forehead and bade me welcome. Cousin Madani ran to meet us and immediately fired a shot in the air as a sign of rejoicing, but my father-in-law scolded him as the family was in mourning for a distant cousin who had been murdered in the Tajmâth that same week. (The police had arrested two notorious criminals who were released after a few days' detention for want of evidence against them.)

I was invited to sit on a thick wool carpet in the midst of a number of women and children. All this bustle around me made me feel quite giddy.

After a moment I began to take in the appearance of the house. Two large buildings stood facing each other, each with a cellar in the basement, above which was one huge room on the ground floor and an upper storey with two balconies. To reach these upper storeys you climbed up a flight of steep steps – more like a ladder – keeping close to the wall of the house as there was no rail to hold on to.

One of these ground-floor rooms was the living quarters for my father-in-law's family; the other was known as 'the storehouse' and contained huge round jars made of plaited alfalfa grass and as high as the ceiling; they must have held five or six hundred measures of corn or barley. During the lifetime of my husband's paternal grandfather, Hacène-ou-Amrouche, they were always filled to the brim.

The courtyard of the house was crowded with men, women and children, who all stared at me relentlessly: I was the stranger, the woman who had taken the favourite son. Meanwhile, a very tall old woman appeared, who was almost blind and walked with the aid of a stick; in spite of her advanced age it was obvious that she had been very beautiful. She came up to my husband, embraced him warmly then she took my head in her hands and kissed me on the forehead. This unexpected expression of affection went straight to my heart.

My husband told me she was his maternal grandmother, Aïni (the mother of Uncle Hemma), who had brought him up and spoilt him!

I entered the large room that served as living quarters for my father-in-law's family. I saw quite a young woman suckling a tiny baby: this was Douda, my father-in-law's second wife. At this time my father-in-law, Ahmed-ou-Amrouche, only had two wives: my mother-in-law, Djohra, who was about forty, and Megdouda, always known as Douda, who seemed very much younger. In addition to Belkacem, my husband, my mother-in-law had two daughters; one, whose name was Ouahchia, was married and lived in a village some distance away. The other one, a thin dark child, was introduced to me: her name was Reskia. Douda had several daughters: the eldest was aged about ten, another one was still a toddler, and then the newborn baby. She told me she also had a son, Mohand-Arab, aged five or six, who lived with his grandfather, Hacène-ou-Amrouche, in Tizi-Aïdhel, a village on the plain, where the old man had retired to live with his two or three wives and his daughter Tassâdith, as far away as possible from his prodigal son. I also noticed a girl who I learned had been brought up in my parents-in-law's home, with the intention of marrying her to their son – she was the fiancée whose place I had taken!

When I arrived my father-in-law went to buy two headscarves with golden stripes (called *cheâla*); he gave one to me and the other to the other girl, as he believed that my husband could love two women, as he did himself.

I was presented to Taïdhelt, the wife of the grandfather in Tizi-Aïdhel, the head of the household and in charge of the old man's money. Her word was law with the whole family. She seemed very sad: her daughter Aïcha had just died from tuberculosis, leaving five orphans, including one suffering from rickets, who was still a baby. Taïdhelt had another daughter, Fatima, who lived near Medjana, so she hadn't yet heard the bad news. She arrived the next day, bringing a pretty little three-year-old girl, Ouardia. She told me she had left her elder son with her husband in Medjana.

To these must be added all the first cousins, their mothers and their wives, who all came, drawn by curiosity.

When night fell my mother-in-law took us to the upper storey, above the small storeroom, where she had prepared our bed: rugs laid out on a rush mat, with a printed cotton sheet to cover us. The room was enormous, over thirty foot long by twenty or twenty-five feet wide. Jars of oil were lined up along the floor at the bottom of every wall, and there were as many in the four other rooms, downstairs as well as upstairs. The windows had heavy shutters that were closed with a sort of wooden bolt: you turned a latch to the vertical position and the bolt shot into the wall into which the window frame was fixed; to open it, you turned the wooden latch back to the horizontal and the bolt fell back; to get in from the outside you'd have had to burn the doors down.

There was no ceiling, so we could see the roof-tiles. There was no comfort, nothing was kept clean and tidy; the floor was paved with bricks, the same as downstairs. Next to us, over the vestibule, Taïdhelt, the grandfather's wife, had her bedroom.

I slept like a log that night. I was so tired! Next morning, it was already late when I woke up. Everybody was busy: Taîdhelt had drunk her coffee and was winding wool on to her distaff; my mother-in-law, Reskia and Hemama, Douda's daughter, as well as my husband's fiancée, had all been out to pick prickly pears, and were setting out the fruit in rows in a shady corner of the courtyard. They had filled up a big wooden dish which anyone could help themselves to at any time; but first you had to pour water over them to blunt the prickles and then cut off the heads and tails with a sharp knife and finally peel off the thick skin.

I watched this procedure with amusement and curiosity. Meanwhile my mother-in-law had taken off the clothes she had worn to pick the fruit and was rubbing herself down hard with a sort of brush made of alfalfa grass, to remove any remaining thorns.

Douda beckoned me over to the hearth, where she stood surrounded by egg-shells. In a large earthenware dish on the fire, a huge *galette* made of very white semolina beaten up with a number of eggs, was frying in oil. This is the traditional breakfast in Aïth-Abbas, reserved for mothers of newborn babies. But that morning Douda had made a mugh bigger *galette* and she gave me and my husband a good quarter of it. She had poured some honey into a bowl and that was our breakfast.

The next day cousin Madani invited us to the midday meal: he had shot a couple of partridges. We went a long way round, through Tahriqth, on the outskirts of the village, so that I should not be seen by people who were not members of the family, to Cousin Chérif's house, as it was called, a large building, consisting of two wings. The older one had been built by Hacène's brother, Mohand-ou-Amrouche, the father of Chérif, Madani and Saïd, who were thus my father-in-law's first cousins. Chérif himself had been responsible for the addition of the other part of the house, on the death of his father. It had a basement, which served as a cellar and stable; the ground floor consisted of one vast room and on the first floor there was another of the same size. Above that again, overlooking the village, was the bed-room for Chérif and his wife, Sassa, whom he had brought back from Aïdh-Aïdhel. I thought that Sassa was very beautiful, in spite of showing the signs of age. She made a delicious *couscous* which she served us in the upper room. From the balcony there was a view over the whole village. I spent the best part of the day in this friendly house; in the evening we returned to my father-in-law's.

On Monday I witnessed a terrible scene: my father-in-law had left early, on his mule, to go to the Akbou market, and in his haste he had forgotten his watch and waistcoat. My mother-in-law, Djohra, had run after him but couldn't catch up with him; so she had entrusted the watch and waistcoat to a wealthy man from the village, Ali-ou-Bouchachi, asking him to give them to my father-in-law. Well, this man, who she'd never have distrusted, kept the watch and chain and the waistcoat.

When Ahmed, my father-in-law, got back from the market, Lla Djohra asked him if the man she'd asked to deliver the watch had done so.

'He didn't give me anything.'

I saw him go out to look for the man in question, who denied receiving anything.

I'll never forget my father-in-law's fury: he was carrying iron stirrups, joined by a leather strap. He seized my mother-in-law by the hair and began to belabour her with all his might. Taïdhelt, Douda, her daughters and I, all rushed up and clung on to his arm to try to make him let go. But he didn't stop beating her till he was exhausted and the strap broke. His eyes were bulging nearly out of their sockets.

Lla Djohra collapsed on the ground.

'That'll teach you to trust strangers,' he said.

At that time, a watch was very precious and a rarity, that was why the man had kept it.

I don't think I spent more than a week at Ighil-Ali. On Tuesday my brother Lämara arrived with two mules. My mother had sent him to Aïth-Mangueleth to fetch me and when he didn't find me there he came on to Aïth-Abbas. We set off almost immediately as my brother had been several days on the road already and the cost of the hire of the mules was mounting up.

I was given ten litres of oil and lots of sweetmeats. Douda made me a semolina *galette* with eggs. I took the lot to my mother.

I didn't stay very long in my home village; I was anxious to get back and get my own affairs in order. At the beginning of September we were back once more in our home in Ouarzen. This was now our daily routine: as soon as we were up we had our breakfast and then went off to the hospital together; at the gate we parted and I went in and made my way to the linen-room where I worked with Sister Chantal until midday. Then my husband came to fetch me. I prepared our meal which we ate together. Father Carisson had bought us some cooking utensils. I'd never learned to cook. I could just about make *afdhir-ou-quessoul* (the pancakes with sauce that the big girls at Taddert-ou-Fella used to make on Sundays), a *galette* and I managed some *couscous*. I still wonder how I ever learned. But I had plenty of common sense and no lack of good will. What is more important, I had watched my mother, who was clean and thrifty as an ant. I paid a woman two francs fifty a month to bring me an eighteen-litre can of water every day. The first time my husband went to market he bought 200 litres of corn – I think he borrowed the money, about twenty francs. He also bought two kilos of meat. I thought it was too much for two people. I salted some pieces to keep, and advised Belkacem not to be so extravagant in future. I was very much my mother's daughter; she always divided the grain into twelve portions, one for every month of the year.

When we had had lunch we went back to the hospital. I worked again till evening, then my husband and I both returned to the house in

Ouarzen. The month of October went by in this way. On 1 November the owner of the house gave us notice, as she said her husband had returned and they wanted the house to themselves. When I entered the linen-room Sister Chantal noticed my red eyes.

'Are you in trouble?' she asked.

Through my sobs I told her that I'd got nowhere to live.

'Don't get upset about that,' she replied. 'I'll arrange something for you.'

She went to see the Mother Superior, who at that time was still Mother Saint-John. Sister Chantal told me, 'I've talked to the Reverend Mother about you; you can have the little room that Amar Akhil was living in; it's vacant now.'

When my husband came to fetch me at midday, I showed him the key, saying, 'The Reverend Mother has given us this room.'

We opened the door and were well pleased. This room was more convenient than the house in the village, and we also had the advantage of not having to go back and forth twice a day. I could get the water we needed from the tap which was a couple of yards away.

We fetched our belongings the same day and that evening we had a place to sleep at last without fear of being made to move. The days slipped past; Father Justrob came back and gave us good advice on making ourselves comfortable; he made us buy planks which could be placed on boxes to serve as a bed. We made shelves out of more planks, which gave us more room. For ten francs or so, we bought a few yards of red flannelette with black stripes to make curtains to hang over the shelves, so that everything was hidden. I got my supplies from the nuns: for sixty centimes I could buy a four-pound loaf, semolina, dried vegetables and coffee. Every week I paid for this out of the money I earned.

Before I left for work in the morning I put my vegetables on to simmer and at nine o'clock Sister Chantal let me go to keep an eye on my fire and my cooking. Every Thursday Uncle Hemma, the caravan-drover, paid us his regular visit. He was very tall and appeared even bigger because of the *guennour* he wore – an imposing turban covered with white muslin, with a brown camel-hair cord wound round it several times to make it even higher. When I knew him he hadn't one tooth in his mouth, nor one single hair on his head. He had a light complexion with fine, regular features, but he had lost the sight of one eye from smallpox and this terrible disease had left his face pitted. The lid of the remaining eye was deformed, turned back to reveal the interior. The first time I saw him all this upset me, then I got used to it.

I would see him coming, every Thursday evening, bringing us all the things he had managed to persuade my parents-in-law to send us by telling them how poor we were. Sometimes it was ten litres of oil, another time a few strings of dried onions. Sometimes he bought us some pomegranates himself, from the market. I made an effort to offer him a good reception, I cooked in his honour a semolina *couscous* or a potato stew into which he dipped huge chunks of fresh black bread that I had got from the nuns.

We didn't go short of anything as life was so cheap that we needed very little money. Whatever I bought from the nuns was calculated at cost price. Every month I got one hundred kilos of oakwood for one franc and whenever my husband had a day off he chopped up a few logs for kindling. I hadn't time to be bored. I was only free on Sundays, then I sometimes went for a walk with the girls who worked for the nuns.

I had taken Félicité's advice and been to see Mme Paquereau, the midwife: she told me I was three months pregnant.

Christmas came. That year I had clogs and really warm slippers. My husband wore a heavy white *burnouse*, as we dresseed in Kabyle fashion at the time. The mission didn't want the Kabyle people to give up their own ways, so the Mother Superior had refused to let me have European shoes and had bought me red leather slippers for my wedding, that the local people call '*thirihith*'.

About this time I had my first real argument with my husband, that nearly ended badly. A man from his village, named Merzoug, had come to work at the hospital, bringing his wife who was expecting a baby. They were living, I think, in the former ironing-room. Well, this man wanted to spend the Christmas holidays at Ighil-Ali, and suggested that my husband go with him. When Belkacem told me about this plan I said that he oughtn't to leave me alone. We argued for a bit and I realised that he really wanted to go. Ever since I had met my father-in-law, Ahmed-ou-Amrouche, I had been afraid he would try to take his son away from me. Then the next day, just as if it had been arranged, my brother turned up. I told him, 'My husband wants to spend a few days with his parents. Take me back with you while he's away.'

I got dressed and we set out on foot. We had already started down the path that leads to the river when I heard my name called. I looked round and saw Father Justrob who was running as fast as he could to catch us up. I stopped and waited for him.

'Why are you leaving?' he asked.

'Because my husband wants to go back to his parents with Merzoug. So I thought, why shouldn't I go and see my mother, too.'

'Merzoug left last night, by himself,' the Father assured me.

And he took me back, keeping an angry eye on my brother till he was well on his way home. We slowly climbed the hill, but I was so exhausted when I arrived, because of the child I was carrying, that I had to go to bed. We never mentioned this incident again.

On 31 December 1899 there was a midnight mass to celebrate the beginning of a new century. It had snowed again. My husband was helping Father Justrob translate the hymns into Kabyle. Those December and January evenings, when night fell quickly, I often worried about Belkacem as I waited for him to return: I was afraid he would fall into a ditch in the snow and freeze.

Sometimes the rain came down the chimney of our room and we couldn't light the fire. We would be reduced to going without supper. Then my husband went to knock at the kitchen door and the nun would offer us some food. She never refused to help us.

On New Year's Day I went with Belkacem to wish the missionaries happy New Year. Father Baldit was now Provincial and had to undertake long journeys to inspect all the mission stations. He used to travel as far as Gardhaïa and would be away for weeks on end, so Father Schmit was now the Superior. He came from Alsace. He was powerfully built and so kind in spite of his severe looks! He loved children. He welcomed us warmly and gave me several bars of chocolate; the other missionaries gave us sweets and sugared almonds. I was really pampered!

I also went to wish the nuns happy New Year, and they were very nice to me too. Sister Chantal, my godmother, gave me a silver medal in memory of her old mother. I returned home with my cheeks as red as tomatoes and my eyes shining with happiness.

When I say 'home' that's just a manner of speaking: it was a room under a low roof made of planks, covered with tiles; it was quite warm because it was raised up and the wooden floor kept it dry. We were very cosy with the curtains we had put up to hide the shelves and our mat and blankets spread out on the bed made of planks. We had boxes to put things on and shoes went under the bed.

I had news of a few of my school-friends from Taddert-ou-Fella: Mahla was at the hospital with her two elder sisters, the two youngest ones were at Ouadhias where they subsequently got married. I met Mme Achab one day when I was out for a walk but as I was a Christian and she was Muslim, she ignored me. One morning the nuns took me to see Alice, who had gone to work as a maid to the Masselot family: the poor girl was so changed that I could scarcely recognise her!

One winter evening I saw another girl arrive with her brother: it was Dabhia who we knew as Maria – she was called by her Kabyle name as well as her French one. She said the Administrator had sent her there to earn her living. M. Masselot was really foisting her on the nuns. She was very impractical – a girl who had read too many books without any discrimination: she was always in a daydream, and with the nuns daydreaming was out!

The Mother Superior agreed to keep Dabhia and she was taken to the linen-room where I worked myself. She slept in the dormitory with the other girls and women. There was plenty of work: besides the mending, we had to do the laundry, the cooking, the ironing; a loom had even been set up and Fatima (the stout one) was weaving a fine *burnouse*, for Father Baldit we thought.

I rarely went by the dormitory since my marriage. I went straight back to my own room as soon as I finished in the linen-room. Meanwhile, more and more girls turned up and the nuns, counting on a good crop of conversions, took some new ones in every day.

Uncle Hemma came regularly to visit us, in all weathers. Once, besides oil, he brought a litre of honey and a kilo of salt butter that Taïdhelt sent, 'for when I had had the baby', she said.

The following week we had a veritable invasion from members of the Amrouche family: Cousin Salah-ou-Amrouche and his wife, accompanied by my sister-in-law, Ouahchia, came to see us on their way back from a pilgrimage to Sheikh Mohand. They all made themselves comfortable in our bed; I made a huge *couscous* with dried meat and a bean soup, of which they all ate their fill. The next morning the cousin and his wife had breakfast of coffee and fresh bread, then left for home, leaving my sister-in-law with us as she wanted to consult the doctor. She had been ill since the birth of her child, six months previously. She lived with us, sleeping in our bed.

One day Father Duchêne happened to drop in; he looked closely at my sister-in-law and then took my husband on one side, saying, 'Antoine,' (that was his Christian name) 'what you're doing isn't healthy or sensible, especially in your wife's present condition.' (I was then eight months pregnant). 'Your sister is consumptive, you only have to look at her eyes to realise it; from now on, you must see that she doesn't sleep in your room any more.'

My husband told me what he had said.

'Come what may,' I replied, 'we can't tell your sister to get out.'

That year, *Mouloud* – the feast of the sheep – fell at roughly the same time as Easter. According to traditional custom, my brother brought me a shoulder of mutton from the sheep that the family had slaughtered. The Christian families had also killed a sheep for Easter and we had a share of that too. I was able to put a good quantity of meat to dry.

Mme Paquereau had helped me make a little layette: a few night-dresses of fine lawn and little flannelette vests; it was all put ready in a trunk that the nuns had given me. I didn't go to the linen-room any more as my feet were swollen, but I did work at home and took it to Sister Chantal. Our friend Habtiche, the second assistant teacher, had been appointed secretary to the mixed commune in Algiers, and had brought me a cloak for the baby I was expecting. From Mme Paquereau I also received two pretty little dresses.

My sister-in-law was still living with us. One Monday there was an eclipse of the sun. At three o'clock in the afternoon the sun disappeared and for a couple of minutes we could see the moon and the stars. Then the sun came out again. Was it the excitement I had felt? I went into labour that same night after the eclipse. Seeing that I was

The house that Fadhma and Belkacem had built in Ighil-Ali, where they lived from 1953 until Belkacem's death in 1959. Photographed in 1960.

Fadhma, aged 18, photographed in 1900 in front of the Amrouche family home in Ighil-Ali, Kabylia, with her first-born son, Paul-Mohand-Saïd.

N° 1053 bis RD

MINISTÈRE
DE L'INFORMATION

Radiodiffusion Française

RÉPUBLIQUE FRANÇAISE

Paris, le 16 avril 45

Ma chère maman,

voici plusieurs semaines que je veux t'écrire une longue lettre. En marchant dans Paris il m'arrive de rêver que tu es à mon bras. Nous allons lentement, très lentement, comme le soir, sur la route le long de la voie du chemin de fer, à Radès. Tu traînes tes pauvres pieds dans tes vieilles savates, tu croises ton fichu décoloré sur ta poitrine mais tes yeux de petite fille malicieuse regardent tout autour, et rien ne leur échappe, des nuances du ciel, des étoiles qui nous font des signes ; une grande paix monte des jardins parmi les parfums qui va se fondre dans la paix qui tombe du ciel.

Et je pense, mélancoliquement, que la vie ne nous accordera plus bien souvent de faire ces promenades, avant que la maison ne replie sur nous ses ailes pour la nuit. Notre maison de Radès, je ne l'évoque jamais sans être ému aux larmes. Elle est si lourde de

J. 23214-44 (16)

Letter from Jean Amrouche to his mother (see pp 191–192).

Maxula Radès   1ᵉʳ Août 1946

Ô mon fils Jean

Je te lègue cette histoire, qui est celle de ma vie, pour en faire
ce qu'il te voudras après ma mort.

Cette histoire est vraie, pas un épisode n'en a
été inventé, toute ce qui est arrivé avant ma naissance
m'a été raconté par ma mère, quand j'ai été à même de le
comprendre. Si j'ai écrit cette histoire c'est que j'estime qu'elle
mérite d'être connue de vous.

Je voudrais que tous les noms propres (si jamais
tu songes à en faire quelque chose) soient supprimés
, et si tu en fais un roman que les bénéfices soient
partagés entre tes frères et ta sœur en tenant compte le me___ de
tes frais et de ton travail.

L'histoire une fois écrite sera cachetée et
remise entre les mains de ton père qui te la remettra
après ma mort.

J'ai écrit cette histoire en souvenir de ma mère tendrement aimée
et de Mᵐᵉ Malaval qui, elle, a m'a donné ma vie Spirituelle

1ᵉʳ Août   31 Août 1946
          M. Amrouche

si je ne pouvais faire éditer ce manuscrit de mon
vivant, je confie le soin exclusif de
le faire éditer sans modifications, ou avec
de légères modifications portant sur la forme,
à ma fille - Marguerite Taos Amrouche, et
à elle seule.
       Paris, le 13 décembre 1964
          M. Amrouche
Marguerite Fadhma Aïth Mansour Amrouche

First page of Fadhma's original manuscript: the letter to her son Jean (see p 193).

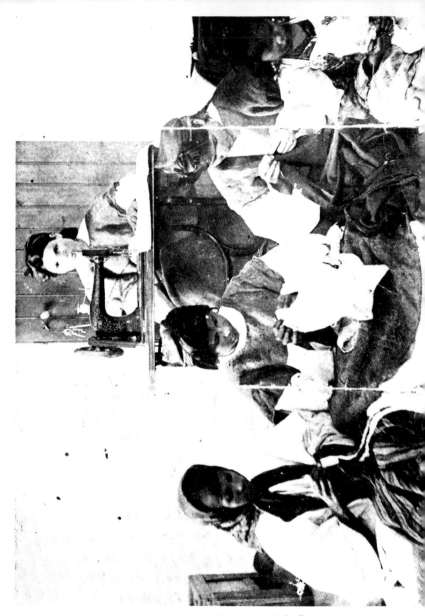

Fadhma, aged 16, at the sewing-machine, with fellow-workers in the linen-room at the Sainte-Eugénie Mission Hospital, in 1898.

Mehed-ou-Merzouk, Belkacem's maternal uncle, in the doorway
of the Amrouche family house in Ighil-Ali. According to Laurence Bourdil,
the women are the Merzouk sisters Aldja and Djohra.

In Tunis (c. 1915), back row:
Henri, Fadhma, Jean, Paul;
front row: Marie-Louise-Taos,
Louis, Belkacem-ou-Amrouche.

Ahmed-ou-Amrouche, Belkacem's
'Prodigal Father', with his
last wife, Zahra (possibly
about 1953, just before his death).

Jean Amrouche with his sister,
Marie-Louise-Taos, in the garden of
the house in Maxula-Radès, 1931,
'the year of the typhoid'.

Two of Belkacem's three Amrouche
cousins (sons of his uncle Mohand-ou-
Amrouche) from the 'Upper Village'.

The Amrouche family in the garden of
their house in Radès: left to right:
Belkacem-ou-Amrouche, Marcel Reggui
(Jean's friend, see p. 146), Noël, Jean
holding Paul's daughter Monique;
in front: Marcel (Paul's son), René.
Possibly 1930–31.

Fadhma Aïth Mansour Amrouche, Paris, 1965 (photo Nicolas Treatt).

**Fadhma with her daughter Marie-Louise-Taos, Brittany,
All Saints' Day (1 November) 1966.**

having pains; my husband persuaded his sister to go and sleep in the women's ward. She grumbled a great deal. At three o'clock in the morning Belkacem went to call the midwife; and my son, Paul-Mohand-Saîd, was born on 29 May 1900.

Sister Chantal came to see me; she brought me some old sheets to use as nappies. Sister Alexis sent an old woman to do my work. Two hens were killed and a *couscous* prepared for the Fathers and the nuns.

As there was no one to look after my sister-in-law who refused to remain in the hospital ward, my husband hired a mule and took her back to Ighil-Ali. He returned two days later.

My mother came to see me; she brought me a present of a huge leg of veal and some eggs; she moved in to take care of me and look after everything. One day when we were alone, she unwrapped the baby's swaddling-clothes and examined the whole of his little body very carefully, and taking note of his feet she said, 'Those feet don't come from our family: our heels don't stick out. He probably gets them from his father's family.'

And as I cried out, 'Be careful you don't hurt him!' she looked over her shoulder at me and retorted, 'Now you're teaching your grandmother how to suck eggs!'

Mme Paquereau had shown me how to bathe the baby and swaddle him.

A few days later my brother came to take my mother home. I got up after two weeks, somewhat thinner. All in all, everything had gone off well.

I resumed my normal activities. We had to leave the room we'd been living in. It had to be demolished to make way for the grand alterations I've already mentioned: a chapel in the basement with living-quarters above it which were to be linked to the existing buildings by balconies.

We were relegated to a room above the stables. It had enormous windows with neither blinds nor shutters and the sun poured in all afternoon, with hundreds of flies as we couldn't shut out the light. The mornings were unbearable and the evenings intolerable. It was summer, July had come round and with it the holiday period. One day my father-in-law, Ahmed-ou-Amrouche turned up with Uncle Hemma.

They escorted us back to Ighil-Ali, riding on mules. The Mother Superior agreed to buy back all the planks we'd bought. Sister Compassion asked for the blankets she'd lent us and I gave them back to her. It didn't take us long to pack up all our belongings. We loaded our little table and our chairs on one of the mules, with my tin trunk and the other trunk. Mme Paquereau wrapped the baby up warmly for the long journey, as we were going to travel through the night.

I said goodbye to Sister Chantal, Mother Saint-John and the whole hospital where I had spent two years, where I had wept, suffered and finally seen my fate settled. From now on, I was no longer alone: for richer or poorer, in laughter or tears, there were now two of us.

On the way we caught up with other people from the village who were on their way home after selling their wool, so we formed quite a caravan along the road. We had set out at three o'clock in the afternoon, when the sun was at its hottest, and didn't arrive till three the next morning. I had been riding on the mule for twelve hours, with my baby in my arms. We had crossed the mountain where it had been very cold, then a river-bed which was nearly dry. When I got down from the mule my legs were so stiff I couldn't move them. The baby was taken out of my arms and I was practically carried into the big living-room. I dropped on to the mat and fell fast asleep.

Ighil-Ali

When I opened my eyes Taïdhelt, grandfather Hacène-ou-Amrouche's wife, was holding the baby in her arms and examining his features closely; he was barely six weeks old.

'He looks like the children of your mother-in-law, Djohra. He's got the same black hair; and he's got their feet and heels.'

I had difficulty standing as my knees ached; I must have caught cold crossing the pass. My husband and I were installed in the storehouse.

With my meagre savings – three hundred francs – I bought some blankets.

The fiancée intended for my husband had gone back to her family, to my father-in-law's great regret. He went to ask the *sheikh* if Koranic law allowed him to marry her himself. But the girl's parents refused to let her become the co-wife of the woman who should have been her mother-in-law.

I tried – not very successfully – to make myself as comfortable as possible in this vast room. I got hold of a round cradle, such as were common in that region, made out of oleander branches and woven cords. We hung it from a beam with a long string attached, so that we could rock the baby. A round rush mat fitted inside as a mattress and the bits of blanket the nuns had given me made do for bedding.

I noticed that everything about this house was quite different from ours: the women were shallow and frivolous, the living-quarters were big but dirty, the floor made of beaten earth was as rough as the day the house was built and the walls which were black with soot were never whitewashed. Jars of oil stood all round the walls. I presumed that the women must spin their wool as at the back of the room there was a loom with a half-woven *burnouse* on it.

There were two sorts of basic food: wheat for the men, barley for the women. I noticed that there was a lot of waste.

My mother-in-law, Djohra, lived in the house with her two daughers: Ouahchia, the one who had come to stay with us at the hospital, died in the September after our arrival; the other one, Reskia, was still only a child. Douda also lived there with her daughters.

My mother-in-law was responsible for the outdoor work, as I had noticed in my visit the previous year, and I was told that this was always the case; so she brought in the prickly pears and the goatskin bottles full of water. She was very sturdy with broad shoulders, rather stockily built, not very intelligent, but with plenty of common sense. When I arrived I wanted to call her 'mother', as was the custom in my village but seeing that she didn't like this, I called her *Lalla* – madame. I shared the *couscous* and *galette* that they all ate, but this food didn't satisfy my husband. He bought some pasta and potatoes and we cooked for ourselves.

*

One morning we saw the entrance gate flung open and a tall man, dressed in a white *burnouse*, led in a heavily laden mule. I still have the sight of this man before my eyes: it was as if he gave off a sort of radiance. He advanced slowly into the courtyard while all the women went to meet him, kissed him on the head and said, '*Aâsslama a Dhada Hacène!*'

I approached shyly in turn and kissed his head which he bent down towards me.

The mule was unloaded. He went upstairs to see his wife, Taïdhelt, whom he called the guardian of his treasures.

My mother-in-law had briefed me: I must see that grandfather gave me some jewellery. The next day I took my baby in my arms and went to present him to his great-grandfather, who was very nice to me. Before I left I timidly asked him for some jewellery; he turned to Taïdhelt and said: '*Efkas ats'sgerouah!* Give her, give her! let her jingle!'

Shortly afterwards he left for Algiers. I learned later that he had gone to welcome home his old friend Boumezrag, the brother of Bach-Agher who had rebelled in 1871; grandfather had known Boumezrag before he was deported for having taken part in the revolt, and was anxious to meet him again now that he'd been released.

Taïdhelt gave me some clasps and a *khelkhal* – an ankle bracelet. Grandfather came back from Algiers a few days later, upset by the change in his friend; he forgot that they had not seen each other for nearly thirty years and that he too had aged.

I could now examine him more closely. He must have been seventy at the time I'm speaking of. His height was increased by the *guennour*, the head-dress of the Aïth-Abbas region. He had a very light complexion, a rather short but well-formed nose, determined chin and a small mouth; although he had lost all his teeth and nearly all his hair, he still had a fine presence. His whole bearing reflected dignity and nobility. I discovered later that the luminosity he radiated was the privilege of those whom God loved.

He left again for Tizi-Aïdhel where he lived all the year round; life was easier there than at Ighil-Ali and the fields were more fertile.

The first unpleasant scene I was involved in was caused by our religion: my husband and I had to go to mass on Sunday mornings. The other Christian families lived close to the mission where the Fathers had built houses for them so that the women could practise their religion without having to go through the village.

According to the customs of Little Kabylia, young women were not allowed to leave their homes and be seen by men. As I was not aware of this, I had prepared clean clothes to go to mass. My mother-in-law saw them laid out over the back of a chair. She rushed out of the room and went to fetch Taïdhelt, whose word was law for the whole household. She was also very well-balanced and knew how to smooth over difficult situations. She asked me what the clothes were for that I had put ready.

'I'm going to church,' I replied. 'You know we are Christians, don't you?'

'It's not proper for a young woman from the Amrouche family to go out in broad daylight and be seen by people in the village: we could never live the disgrace down; we'd be the laughing stock of everyone and our family is very powerful and of high standing.'

'What am I supposed to do then?' I replied. 'I must go to church, it's obligatory for me too.'

'You'll have to get up before the men are at their early-morning prayers and not return till it is dark, so that nobody in the village will be able to say you've been seen going to the *Roumis*.'

There was nothing for it but to obey. For years we got up before dawn and slipped away secretly. The nuns opened the door as soon as they heard me knock and let me in to the classroom. As long as Mother Madeleine was the Superior, she always let me eat with the boarders that she had at the time.

Whenever there was some serious reason for me to get back early – if the child was ill, for example – we used to take a long roundabout way through the fields, and when I got home I was aware of their hostile glances. I was the renegade, who had denied her religion and cast a spell on the favourite son.

There was one charming old lady among all these women, who had accepted me without any reservations: this was Lalla Aïni, my husband's maternal grandmother. She had declared to her daughter, Lalla Djohra, 'From now on your daughter-in-law will be my daughter instead of you; I shall invite her whenever an opportunity occurs.'

She kept her word; she was always ready to help me or stand up for me when I was in difficulties.

There were two distinct clans in this family. On the one hand there were the 'valley Amrouches' – my father-in-law's family – and on the other, the 'upland Amrouches' – grandfather Hacène's wives and daughters. The latter had to have precedence no matter what the circumstances, for, when all was said and done, it was grandfather Hacène who supported this whole hornets' nest, and it was his wife, Taïdhelt, who held the purse-strings.

The valley family was jealous of the upland family and the latter looked down their noses at the former, thinking them lucky – rightly or wrongly – to be linked to them at all.

One day in the summer of 1900 bad news was brought to Taïdhelt; her son-in-law, Lärbi-ou-Herrouche, had been found drowned in a place called Ras-el-Oued, not far from where he had a provision store; he also used to sell lengths of material to Arabs. His body had been found in an isolated spot where he had gone to perform his ablutions before praying.

The authorities gave a verdict of accidental death. He was brought back to the village but it was at the height of summer and the body had been in the water for some time and was already all bloated, so he had to be buried the same evening. So Fatima, my father-in-law's sister, was now a widow and a few months later she came back to live with the family. She had three children; the eldest, a boy, had slept near his father's corpse and contracted a high fever. For several days his life hung by a thread. The little girl, Ouardia, was three and the youngest barely twelve months old.

With all these extra people, the house was really overcrowded. So then my father-in-law decided to put up another building, next to the oil-press. He engaged bricklayers and in the course of 1900-1901 they erected what was known as 'the new house' and 'the new upper storey'.

The summer of 1900 was stifling and the women slept out of doors, on sheets spread out on the bare ground in the courtyard. My father-in-law slept on one of the two stone benches in the vestibule, built for this purpose. I slept in the storehouse where my son Paul's cradle hung. We had a rush-mat on which we spread a camel-hair rug which was used for riding the mule and on market days we had to give up this rug and go back to sleep on the mat and sheet; but we were so young!

In September my sister-in-law, Ouahchia, died from tuberculosis; they had had to cut her hair short as she was covered in lice. She had lost so much weight she was quite unrecognisable. But Lalla Djohra declared that her daughter had been poisoned by her co-wife, accusing her of giving her daughter *ihechcoulen* to eat – food she had cast a spell on, including monkey droppings . . . That was why, according to her, the poor girl looked like a monkey before she died . . . However hard I tried to explain to my mother-in-law that her daughter had died from a disease that had not been treated properly, like the majority of the Amrouche daughters (before Ouahchia, so they told me, there had been her aunt Aïcha, Dahbia, Negdouda and quite a few others), Lalla Djohra insisted her daughter had been poisoned and she made her son-in-law get rid of the woman he had married before Ouahchia.

In the village a girl had just been repudiated, and as her father belonged to our clan, Taïdhelt, with grandfather's permission,, paid back the dowry due to the husband. This girl, Zahra T'Gouarab, was said to be very beautiful and my father-in-law decided to marry her. He couldn't manage it that year and she was promised to a man from a neighbouring village who put up a large dowry for her; and for some time that was the last we heard of the matter.

The olive season came round. That's the time in Ighil-Ali when the women are rushed off their feet as, old or young, they all have to go out olive-picking. They'd be up before dawn, decked out in all their finery, their faces made up, wearing their scarlet *babouches* embroidered with black stitching, adorned with all their jewellery, and off they'd go to the fields. These women really enjoy the olive season as it's the only time they can leave the house. When they get home, exhausted but happy, the stars are already out.

For me, that was a terrible year, the worst that I experienced in that house. As all the women helped with the olive-picking, it was my job to look after the house, sift the two basketfuls of grain that had to be ground during the night and prepare the evening meal. I had to start work very early: the baskets were enormous, one of barley for the women and labourers, the other of wheat for the men of the family. My mother-in-law and Douda, her co-wife, cooked the *galettes* that they took out with dried figs for the midday meal and something to eat in the afternoon.

I had to look after Paul who had just turned six months and I hadn't the strength for all this work, which I wasn't used to either. However I made an effort to please everybody. Grandmother Aïni came every day to keep me company. As she was nearly blind she couldn't be of much real use to me. She would rock Paul in his cradle but when she wanted to pick him up he started to scream as he was afraid of her closed eyes. First I picked over the grain, then I prepared breakfast for my husband who was teaching at the mission; after that I took the enormous wooden dish that was used for rolling the *couscous*, and I rolled and rolled, filling up the strainers; then I lit the fire and put the lot on to cook. Then when night fell and the oil-lamp was lit, Lalla Djohra and Douda served everyone: the labourers in the vestibule, the men of the family separately, and finally the women and children who gathered round the big ashwood bowl, on its stand.

The days went by. October, then November, then December. Christmas came round. The olives were picked, the little girls of the family could then go and collect for themselves any left behind: sometimes the mothers left some olives on purpose . . .

That Christmas I slept over at the convent: they had invited me to have supper with their boarders. I spent the day with them, with the other Christian families. The next day when it was quite dark, I returned home.

Belkacem earned fifty francs a month from the Fathers. With this meagre sum we thought we could afford to pay for the roof, the ceiling, the floor-tiles and plastering for the new upper storey that my father-in-law was building, as with the innocence of youth, we thought that this was going to be our permanent home!

My husband sent to Bougie for roofing-tiles and battens, flooring-tiles and window-panes, which he paid for himself. I learned later that he'd had to borrow money for this. I continued to eat with the rest of the family, but I always kept some bread, a tin of sardines and some camembert cheese in my trunk. Sometimes, on Saturday evenings,

Belkacem even got M. Jean, the mission cook, to roast a piece of meat for us.

My mother-in-law, Djohra, had another brother besides Hamma; his name was Khaled and he was already quite old, bald and toothless. He was tall and dried up as a piece of wood, he had regular features and an intelligent appearance: like his brother Hemma, he gave the impression of being the last of a line.

Khaled had married his first cousin, an orphan who had been brought up by grandmother Aïni. For reasons unknown to me, Khaled had broken away from the rest of the family in 1900, and they were all inconsolable, especially his mother. His wife had had several children, all lovely babies, as she was very beautiful, but none of them had lived for twelve months. As soon as they began to crawl, or even to sit up against a wall, they were carried off by some incurable disease. I was present when the last one died within a few days, a child I'd seen the picture of health: he had even lost his sight before he died.

Mother and son sometimes met at our house. One day I was horrified to witness one of their quarrels: the blind mother, Lalla Aïni, reproached her son for having deserted her and Khaled retorted that he was sick of working for her and his brother and sister. The quarrel became more acrimonious. Khaled finally flung at her, 'When you die, I'll defile your grave!'

I can still see the terrible look on the old woman's face as she pointed a finger at her son accusingly and cried, '*Roh a Khaled ammi, ak yefk Rebbi i yibherdan idheyqen d' chbhabhat iremqen!*' Which means, 'May God see to it, Khaled my son, that you pass through a narrow way and find yourself face to face with cunning enemies!'

They never saw each other again. Three years later, to the old woman's despair, they brought back the body of this son she had loved so much: the curse had been fulfilled, he had been killed by cunning enemies who had ambushed him in a narrow defile. One day as he was coming back from the Aïth-Warlis market on his mule, with his rifle on his shoulder, he must have been followed by an enemy, or come upon unexpectedly by a criminal: he had been shot through the head, the bullet passing through one eye and coming out at the back of his neck.

*

The customs at Ighil-Ali were different from those where I came from. For example, for a death, there was no *sadhaqa* – that is, the sacrifice of an animal – as in my village; all they did, if they could afford it, was to prepare a lavish meal for the strangers who came from neighbouring regions to present their condolences.

There was no community spirit in the family, it was everyone for themselves; often, after Taïdhelt had gone to bed, Douda and my mother-in-law climbed on to the jar of wheat and helped themselves to two or three measures that they later sold and shared the money from; it was the same with the sacks full of barley flour that grandfather Hacène sent us from Tizi-Aïdhel, where he owned land. Besides which, both of them and especially my mother-in-law had poor relations they helped to the best of their ability. Flour, oil, *galette* or *couscous* were all given away disproportionately; Taïdhelt herself fed the children of her widowed daughter, Fatima.

Wool was the most important business in Ighil-Ali. The men travelled great distances to the towns in the south, to buy heavy loads of wool; they went as far as Ouargla, Djelfa and Laghouat, passing through Aumale and Msila. They would leave on a Wednesday taking a *galette*, some figs and olives and a goatskin of water to eat and drink on the way. They didn't get back till Saturday evening, exhausted from the long journey through the desert. Others, who had a bit of capital, set up in trade in Tizi-Ouzou, Orleansville, Miliana or Batna. They returned when the first frosts set in, and bought stocks of corn for the winter with the profits they had made.

The women, for their part, spent the months from spring through to autumn, weaving *burnouses*; they or their husbands sold these and the money went for household expenses.

Lla Djohra, my mother-in-law, told me that when she was young and Hacène-ou-Amrouche and his son Ahmed still lived together, the women had to be up before daybreak; some of them settled down to grinding, others to weaving, while the old grandfather sat by the fire and was served with cups of hot coffee. My mother-in-law used to sleep very soundly after her hard day's work, so she had to beg Taïdhelt to wake her up in the mornings.

When once the grandfather had left, the women had more freedom, but they still had to weave *burnouses*, like all the women in the village. The profit on these was very small, but they never remained inactive.

The men who didn't have enough money to buy wool made carding combs. This only needed a small outlay, and they didn't take up much room. That's what Lla Djohra's father did; as long as his eyes were good enough, he made carding combs all the week and on Mondays he took them all to market, thirty kilometres on foot, there and back . . .

The soil around Inghil-Ali is very poor; there is a lot of shale and very little cereals can be grown so people had to wait impatiently for market day to get in fresh supplies. I found a great difference from my village of Tizi-Hibel; my mother never had to buy anything; even the cattle were fattened up at home.

In winter, when the river was high enough to turn the mill-wheel the little mill-house was opened up and the villagers brought their grain to be ground. Rabah, a distant cousin who worked for us and was kept by the family, looked after this mill and was paid in flour. For several winters running we had plenty.

It was now the spring of 1901. The olives had all been pressed and a good quantity stored in the oil-jars. But what a lot was wasted! Even the children rushed off to the oil-press to collect the oil that was running away, so that they could sell it on their own account.

My father-in-law, Ahmed, took no interest in anything useful. He sat around in the café from morning to night, and though he provided food for the labourers, he left them to go off to the fields without any supervision and to work or not as they pleased. One day he went to Tizi-Aïdhel to drive back two mules laden with corn. At the pass, known as Col de Pierre, one of the mules lost its footing and fell down a ravine. It was the chestnut-coloured one that grandfather Hacène was very fond of, that he called Gazelle.

The man Zahra T'Gouârab had got engaged to died, so my father-in-law declared that he wanted to marry her himself. The marriage took place in December 1901. It was a grand wedding, with musicians coming up from the plain. The festivities lasted several days. When the seven days of ritual rejoicing were over, Zahra took her place with the other wives. And each one of the three had her turn to spend the night with my father-in-law in the new house. But Doud insisted she ought to have the same trousseau as the new bride. So she left her young daughters in Ighil-Ali and went back to her parents. But as she was expecting a baby that same month, Taïdhelt went to fetch her back as it was not proper for her to give birth in her parents' house.

My mother-in-law Djohra and Douda had set up a fine white woollen *burnouse* on the loom for their joint husband, Ahmed-ou-Amrouche, but seeing that he had married Zahra, they decided to abandon the work, insisting that it was now the new wife's job to finish the weaving. And what a mess she made of it! At the time, my father-in-law was a little over forty. He was of medium height, but his *guennour* made him look quite tall. He was very dark, with tawny, deep-set eyes; he had a beard and moustache. He looked very fierce to me and I didn't like being near him.

Paul was walking now. He was a lovely child with fair curly hair and enormous golden-brown eyes. The whole family made a fuss of him as there were very few boys among the Amrouches. Even the villagers spoilt him and everyone in the neighbourhood knew *Poupoul-ou-Amrouche*, as they called him. We were living in the new upper storey that we had helped to build, a large rectangular room with four windows and two doors, one opening out on to the balcony and the other on to the little terrace. The windows were glazed (not just with shutters like the other room) and the fireplace was decorated with mosaics. We were very comfortable in summer, but froze in winter as the chimney smoked.

I had taken sides with my mother-in-law when all the household ganged up against the new bride, Zahra, who enjoyed many privileges, so they said. I ought to have remained neutral but I was still very young. Yet, Zahra hadn't done me any harm and she often carried Paul about on her back.

The months went by. It was spring again. Douda had given birth to another daughter and had gone back to her own family, and my mother-in-law Djohra had herself gone to stay with her relatives. The level of corn in the alfalfa jars was diminishing visibly. Taïdhelt had allowed my father-in-law to marry Zahra, as a punishment for Douda and my mother-in-law; they had complained to her own co-wife (Hacène-ou-Amrouche's second wife) about her feeding her daughter's fatherless children and all her other grandchildren, to the two women's detriment. So grandfather Hacène had removed the running of the household from her hands; whereupon she said, 'I shall plant a bramble bush near their hearth!' That meant that they had an enemy.

It was now 1902. I had quarrelled with Zahra who had tried to order me about. I declared that from now on I wouldn't stay in the family house and withdrew with my husband and child to our own quarters. When summer came we all three went to visit grandfather in Tizi-Aïdhel. His daughter Aïcha was born about that time: he had recently taken a new young wife and this was her first child. He had remarried a score of times, on the pretext that a wife saves the cost of a servant, but he also hoped to have a second heir, to put a stop to his eldest son's extravagances – my father-in-law being completely improvident, always spending money without ever earning any.

Hacène-ou-Amrouche made us very welcome. His household consisted of his second wife, a woman well on in age, their daughter Tassâdit, and the new young wife who had just had the baby. Cousin Madani went with us, for family reasons. We stayed there for two days and the third day, when we rode back on our mules, we were given gifts and a *fellah* as an escort.

Taïdhelt had been instructed to let us have our share of the corn; I had a little stock of oil; for the rest, my husband earned enough for us to live on. I had a miscarriage and was weak for a long time; I was able to get up at last, and as the olive season had come round, I went with the other women to help with the picking. I found it very painful to walk when the ground was so hard from the frost, but since the others managed, why shouldn't I?

In the Amrouches' alleyway there were three other houses, besides ours, belonging to my father-in-law's first cousins, and another one where the Ifetouhen family lived. The alley was closed off at night by a heavy gate, similar to the one that led to the vestibule and each of the houses had its own courtyard protected by an identical gate.

In one of these houses lived a certain Salah-ou-Amrouche whose mother's name was Yamina T'ouêla, but the children used to call her Touêla. She was very jolly and very ugly, with one squint eye; she was black and shrivelled up like a wooden stake. She lived by pilfering and scrounging, gathering olives from fields where the owners were absent or busy elsewhere. Our family had a soft spot for her and never refused her anything she asked for. She was in the habit of begging my husband for a couple of pence to buy snuff, that she claimed she needed for her health. In summer, she went out to the prickly-pear plantations during the siesta, and came back with heavy basketfuls that she put to dry for the winter.

I also enjoyed the company of my husband's grandmother, Aïni. She would recount all the ramifications of the Amrouche and Merzouk families. She told me that the house we were living in had been, up to 1871, the property of the four Merzouk brothers, whose mother, although blind, was a very energetic woman who kept the family together. She said she had known grandfather Hacène-ou-Amrouche when he was still a boy: he was the third son of a woman who came from Taqorabth who had been left a widow with five sons: Mohand, Hacène, Tahar, Lhoussine and Chérif.

I learned that she herself came from a well-to-do family and that her parents used to give her wheat-cakes, figs and a sweetmeat called *the-zemith* (made of toasted barley-flour, olive-oil and sugar) that she shared among her children. And Hacène-ou-Amrouche, who was still a child at that time, would also get a generous share. He was in the habit of lying on his stomach making carding combs and one day, when thus occupied, he fell asleep and shouted out in a dream, 'Catch my horse! Catch my horse!' Then he woke up with a start, saying, 'Where is it? Where's the horse?' And Aïni answered, 'You've been dreaming, my little Hacène. There's no horse!'

Ever since that day he got the idea of enlisting with the *Roumis*. When he was eighteen he joined the *spahis* (the Algerian cavalry serving with the French army) at Bordj-bou-Arreridj, and that's how he made his fortune.

Old Taïdhelt told me the rest of the story: cavalryman Hacène-ou-Amrouche quickly gained promotion and when he had learned French he became an interpreter. After several previous wives, he married Taïdhelt, who was very young at the time. They lived in a big house in the city. Grandfather got to know a number of Arabs from whom he rented several fields; he sowed them with wheat and used the army horses for threshing the grain: they threshed during the night and at daybreak he washed them down at the drinking-trough and took them back to the stables, as fresh as if they had not spent the night on the threshing-floor. And that, according to Taïdhelt, is the way he amassed a fortune. In his home all the wives wove wool, as grandfather insisted on everyone working.

He had taken part in the Crimean War and called Sebastopol 'The City of Bronze'. He didn't return to Ighil-Ali till 1871. His exile had lasted thirty years, Taïdhelt emphasised. He obtained a concession from the government, which he sold. He had served in the army for twenty-one years.

Hacène-ou-Amrouche settled in his native village with his wives and children. He acquired extensive olive groves, a fig plantation and another of prickly pears. He still had a little money over and this he lent out to financially sound farmers at a reasonable interest.

At that time, my father-in-law, Ahmed, must have been about twelve. According to his grandmother Aïni he was tall for his age, very thin and dark-skinned. He was very spoilt and was nicknamed *aêggoun* – the idiot – because he spoke a garbled mixture of Arabic and Kabyle; when the family went out olive-picking he had a tiny little basket and every time it was full his father gave him a penny; the women used to fill up Ahmed's basket behind Hacène-ou-Amrouche's back, so that he would get more pennies! But it seems to me that this just prevented the lad from getting a taste for work.

When his son was a bit older, Hacène-ou-Amrouche married him to a girl from the village, Douda. And at the same time as his son married Douda, he, the father married her elder sister, so there was a double wedding on the same day.

My father-in-law's bride, who was still a child, didn't want to stay with him; she went back to her parents where she remained for seven years. When she returned my father-in-law had married a distant cousin, Djohra (my mother-in-law), Lârbi-ou-Merzouk's daughter. There were, it appears, epic quarrels between the two co-wives, with Douda's elder sister – the one who was married to Hacène – taking her part. The wool was divided between them and they each had to weave a *burnouse*: it was a race between them to be the first to prepare the wool, so as to get the best place to set up the loom. Well, Douda got help from her sister, from Taïdhelt and the latter's daughters, while Lalla Aïni and an aunt lent my mother-in-law a hand, but she always got the worst of it as she already had children to look after (my husband and another boy who died in infancy, probably for lack of adequate care).

Grandfather Hacène didn't think much of his son, nor his daughters-in-law; he used to call them '*rehbet-l'emcassir*' (the tribe of weaklings); according to him, both women were lazy.

He divorced Douda's sister and brought in a very young bride from Aïth-Aïdhel, then another from the same region, an extremely beautiful girl called Ouardia – the rose.

Mohand-ou-Amrouche, Hacène's elder brother, Madani's and Chérif's father, had just died. Chérif, then aged fifteen, took over the running of the estate and, disregarding his uncle's advice and caution, indulged in one wild extravagance after another. As was customary, Hacène-ou-Amrouche married his brother's widow to try to halt the damage, but it was too late. Chérif came back from Aïth-Aïdhel with a wife who was extremely beautiful but who had a reputation for easy virtue. However, from the time she arrived in Ighil-Ali her behaviour was above reproach. The days went by. Chérif's and Madani's mother left Hacène-ou-Amrouche and went to live with her sons. Hacène paid off the debts but took as security one of the best fields belonging to his dead brother's heirs: this was *Ighil*.

About this time, when his grandson Belkacem-ou-Amrouche was still quite small, Hacène put him in the care of his maternal grandmother Aïni, as he was afraid the other women would harm him. When he was a bit bigger, he handed him over to the White Fathers who took him as a boarder.* He himself left Ighil-Ali together with his wives, to live at a distance from his son Ahmed, of whom he said, 'His hands are made to spend money instead of earning it.'

He lived for some years with a tribe called *Izenaguen*, then he went to settle in Tizi-Aïdhel, the area where one of his wives (Tabhoutihth) came from and where he bought, as well as taking as security, properties extensive enough to allow him and his family to live comfortably. He handed over the properties in Ighil-Ali, together with the house and the oil-press, to his son Ahmed.

---

* We know that Fadhma's husband, Belkacem, was christened by the Fathers at the age of five. This would have been approx. 1886 (D.S.B.).

That was the state of affairs with the Amrouche family when I arrived in 1900.

The Death of Grandfather Hacène-ou-Amrouche and the Decline of the Family

I have always enjoyed the company of old people; they were always helpful and of good counsel to me, the stranger, the exile. So, it was Taïdhelt who suggested that I learn to weave, so that I could make clothes for my children, who, as she said, are not born fully clad. She even washed a fleece of wool for me, combed and carded it and I learned to spin.

My mother came to visit me; she spent a fortnight in my father-in-law's house, and Douda liked her very much and couldn't do enough for her. My mother was a real busy-bee; she finished weaving the *burnouse* that had been on the loom for more than a year and which none of my father-in-law's wives, neither the two older ones nor the new young one, wanted to work on. When the two weeks were up she went home. My brother Lâmara came to fetch her, saying everything was going wrong in the house since she'd been away.

I did my best to make her stay happy. Douda and my mother-in-law gave her fritters and Taïdhelt presented her with ten litres of oil; I added a measure of corn and a sheet. She and my brother were well pleased.

That was the first and last time that I was to have my mother to stay in that house.

The summer of 1903 came round. I could now weave and I made woollen *burnouses* to sell at the market. My mother-in-law Djohra had left her husband's house for good and was living with us, on the upper floor of the big house.

Both she and her co-wife Douda – and especially the latter – had consulted all the soothsayers and sorcerers to try to make my father-in-law turn against Zahra and repudiate her; they spent enormous sums on spells and even went so far as to bury a bone from a decaying carcase under his bed, but it was all to no purpose, he still loved her. She had already borne him two daughters, of which the first one had died.

My husband decided to apply to the Government for a job as primary school teacher, to get better pay and be eligible for a pension. I wrote a pathetic letter to the Director of Schools for the region, but Belkacem was the victim of discrimination, because of his religious convictions. When he went to see the inspector in Sétif, he was told bluntly, 'If you want to go in for teaching, you can't be a practising Catholic.' My husband had refused to give up his religion and returned home with nothing to show for his pains.

On the very same day he returned, 8 September, my son Henri-Achour was born at three o'clock. Paul was three. His grandfather held the gun for him so that he could fire a shot as a sign of rejoicing. The occasion was celebrated with a feast such as I've never seen since. All the women of the village, young and old, came to congratulate me and join in the dance: one woman beat out the rhythm on a paraffin drum, others accompanied her by clapping and singing, while others danced and chanted 'The Cry of Joy' – 'Oh, you whose joy I have shared, come now and rejoice with me!' No one returned home till late in the evening.

I received gifts from all around: eggs, quarters of sheep, flour and even honey. The house was so full of presents that my mother-in-law didn't know where to put them all. A huge ceremonial *couscous* had been prepared and all our friends flocked to share it with us; we even sent some to friends' houses where there were sick people or women who had also just given birth.

Khaled-ou-Merzouk, who had been given the responsibility of sharing out the meat among the guests, didn't even keep a single bit for himself. I offered him a piece of honey cake that I had been given. I shall always remember that night.

Sometimes the nuns came to visit me when they were passing through.

I made them as welcome as I could. Once Sister Suzanne – the nun from Ouadhias – came to see me. She had aged and her face was quite shrivelled. She told me that she had just come from Tagmount and when I asked her for news of my mother, she informed me that she had got dropsy which was a lie, but she was still at pains to upset me!

My sister-in-law, Reskia, was now getting married. Her in-laws didn't spare any expense: they brought a sheep 'on the hoof', as they say locally. Huge quantities of snow-white *couscous* were prepared with a bright red sauce and lots of onions. There was a drummer and musicians who played 'Kiss me Ninette' on the clarinet, a tune that was popular at the time with the French. The celebrations went on all night and all the women danced, with my father-in-law joining in too. The next day the bride, dressed in the richest garments from her trousseau, accompanied by the women in their holiday finery and the men shouldering their rifles, set off on a mule, bedecked in silken trappings, for the village which was several kilometres away, where the wedding celebrations would continue. My mother-in-law went with her daughter and would not return, according to custom, till the seventh day.

But on the seventh day both my mother-in-law and her daughter returned, as the latter had started having fits of hysterics. The sight of her collapsing on the ground, shrieking wildly, gave me the shivers, as it brought back memories of a school-fellow at Taddert-ou-Fella who had to be dismissed because she terrified the whole school. She was very dark, with huge, gleaming eyes and a scar right across her lip and sometimes, no matter where she was, she would roll her eyes like a madwoman, fling out her arms and shout, 'Dhada Hamou! Dhada Hamou!' and fall down in a heap. I learned that this man she was talking about was an uncle who had terrorised her. Because of this the headmistress had to send her away.

The sight of my sister-in-law Reskia reminded me of this episode from my childhood. Her mother moved her into the old upper storey above the big house. The room was very large, but the low roof made it feel quite snug; the floor was of beaten earth. There was a fireplace where we cooked our meals. When the girl's fits began again, for no apparent reason, it needed four or five women to hold her down, some securing her feet, others her arms, and her head rolled from side to side while she screamed for nearly an hour.

Father Dehuisserre came to see my sister-in-law, Reskia. He suggested a change of air. Local *marabouts* (holy men) were also called in, one old man in particular – Sidi Tahar Aïth Boundaouth: he came to exorcise the poor girl who, he said, was possessed by demons. One day she set off with her mother, Lla Djohra, and my father-in-law to go to consult a famous *marabout*: Sidi Yehya Bel Djoudi. This *marabout* had the power to expel the particular demon which seizes on young brides and tortures them; many girls from the village had been cured of this trouble after staying a couple of days in his hermitage, a holy place where all wretched folk could find food and shelter.

They set off one morning on the mules that belonged to the family; but they were caught in the snow in the Boni forest and had to shelter with the forest keeper who had stayed with us during the summer. They returned two days later, delighted with the reception by Sidi Yeyha. He had promised my sister-in-law an immediate cure and she was soon able to walk properly on the soles of her feet, whereas ever since her wedding she'd been walking on her heels.

It was during November of that same year that the tragic death occurred of my mother-in-law's brother, Khaled-ou-Merzouk. He used to ride his mule from market to market, with his rifle slung over his shoulder to sell his wool. But one day he did not return at the same time as the other merchants. His wife waited for him in vain till nightfall. Then she hurried to her brother-in-law Hemma's house and called all the men of the family out to go and look for Khaled.

They found the unfortunate man lying across the path. A bullet had pierced one eye and emerged at the back of his neck. His mule was still standing next to him and his load had not been tampered with; only his rifle was missing. The law officers came and held the inquest on the spot; they opened the stomach, which was empty as it was the time of fasting. The men returned towards the morning, escorting the body which lay across the mule. They made their way to the parents' house and laid the body on the ground. I shall never forget the scene which ensued: the blind mother groping her way to find her beloved son's wound. First she put her hand on the empty eye-socket, then felt for the hole that the bullet had made as it emerged at the back of the neck. Then she went back to her bed from which she never rose again. God had indeed listened to the curse that the mother had uttered three years before. (Her son had indeed been found 'in a narrow lane, face to face with cunning men'). Her blind eyes wept till they had no more tears to shed.

Grandfather Hacène came from Tizi-Aïdhel in time for the funeral: he grieved deeply as he loved the dead man and found him very intelligent and of good counsel. I myself wept bitterly for this man who had been most helpful to me (he and his wife would refuse me nothing; often the latter would leave her loom to make me some dish I was fond of). The widow went to live with her father-in-law; then, as she was still young, she remarried.

1904 was particularly disastrous for us.

My sister-in-law had no more hysterical attacks, so she went back to her husband. There were more weddings in the house, with more musicians, more drums, dancing and rejoicing. But the situation with my father-in-law, Ahmed-ou-Amrouche, went from bad to worse. That man squandered money like water, but he never earned a penny and his wives accused him of philandering; they noticed that whenever he went to collect the interest on the money owing to his father in the villages, he took presents intended for women. Moreover, he gambled at cards and as he was a bad player, there were always some rogues who managed to cheat him.

He had run up debts for which he had offered the house at Ighil-Ali as security. Feeling himself getting on in years, Hacène-ou-Amrouche had given his son power of attorney, which allowed him to act on his behalf with his creditors. The olive crop had been very good and the contents of some of the jars had had to be sold so that they could be filled with fresh oil.

It was May when grandfather Hacène learned that his house had been given as security (and that during his own lifetime!). There must have been a terrible scene and my father-in-law, who was afraid of his father, beat a retreat. The old man came down from Tizi-Aïdhel one Saturday morning. He asked for the upper storey, where we lived, to be swept and cleaned, ordered a copious *couscous* and summoned his son's creditor, a man from a wealthy family in the plain. The *cadi* was at the market that day. Grandfather paid off the debt but withdrew the power of attorney from his son, who was henceforth dependent on Taïdhelt's goodwill.

The village was very lively at this time. Merry songs reached us from around the oil-presses, where flocks of little girls gathered between six and seven o'clock, each with a baby on her back – a little sister, brother, nephew or cousin. They set their charges down on the ground and sang and clapped, scarlet as cockerels. Some of the little girls beat time on paraffin tins while the others danced. During the important festivals, like the festival of the sheep, they arranged their own little feasts: some would bring meat, others red pepper, some flour or onions. Fires were lit, the bigger ones rolled the *couscous* and the youngsters had a real party. I often watched them from my window, smiling to see all this happiness that I had never known myself. My young sisters-in-law, Reskia and Hemama, and later Tchabha and Zehoua in their time, all took part in these games and merrymaking and sometimes, when they came home in the evenings, drunk from all the sunshine, singing and dancing, they would fall asleep before they had even had their supper. These little girls formed rival gangs associated with the different oil-presses, and amused themselves shouting insults from one press to another; the girls from Aïth-ou-Samer and those from Tirilt had been enemies from time immemorial and would hurl abuse at each other. With Zehoua, in particular, there were no half measures in the quarrels with the youngsters opposite.

I was not unhappy. However, I had to show my teeth on one or two occasions when one of the boys in the family tried to hit Paul. I insisted that my son fight back in whatever way he could, punching, scratching, biting and, if he was getting the worst of it, by throwing stones. Fatima didn't approve as her son, Mekhlouf, being Taïdhelt's grandson, belonged to the 'upland family', whereas we, through our relationship to my father-in-law, were the 'valley Amrouches', which meant that we had to put up with the whims of the others. I made it clear to Fatima that my son would stand up for himself the best way he could, and if she didn't like it, she knew who she would have to deal with: she just had to try going for me and I'd hit back. And we heard no more of the matter.

Many of the village women, whose children had left for the city, came to see me and I wrote letters for them and read them the ones they received and provided them with paper and envelopes if they didn't have any. Some of these women brought me eggs. When they expressed the wish that I 'inherit all the wealth of the Amrouche house', I would reply, 'May the Lord open a door for me to depart from this house!'

On 13 June 1904 I was busy making the *couscous* to take to the nuns and the Fathers, as I did every year on Saint Anthony's Day, my husband's patron saint. Tears streamed from my eyes and my nose was running like a tap. I went downstairs and asked Douda to help me as my head was throbbing. Douda made me lie down and said she would take care of the meal. I lay down in a corner of the old house, under the cradle, the place kept for anyone who was ill. I was consumed with fever and my father-in-law had brought home some ice that the mountain folk had found in a crevasse and sold at the market. He made me some iced lemonade. I drank this greedily and went back to bed. My son Henri was nine months old, I had to drop everything. Douda took care of me and the child.

Father Dehuisserre came a few days later, he diagnosed pleurisy. He applied a number of cupping glasses, then blistered me and my temperature went down. My healthy appetite was my salvation. Every morning and evening I ate my fill of cutlets and fried eggs. I was ill for two weeks. Henri must have been breast-fed by women of doubtful cleanliness, he had lost weight and had sore eyes.

Father Dehuisserre had set up a bed for me on trestles with a straw mattress. When I was a little better, he said, 'I don't want you to sleep down here any more, I've seen too many die in this corner!'

When at last I could get up I decided to go to Saint Eugénie Hospital for a change of air and to convalesce. My husband found a cart – a cross between a wheelbarrow and a hand-cart. My mattress was installed on it. The last straw was when Paul fell on to a sharp stone and cut his forehead badly. Father Dehuisserre had to stitch the wound up.

So we all set off on this cart, my husband, the children and myself, accompanied by a distant cousin. We had to travel by night, because of the heat, as it was at the beginning of July.

We arrived at Michelet at daybreak and were made welcome by our friend Habtiche, who was now employed as a clerk for the mixed commune of Michelet. We rested at his house and then I wanted to go on to the hospital. I thought that, as a protégée of the nuns, they would give me room.

At the hospital I asked for Mother Compassion, the Mother Superior. I explained my situation to her. She looked at me closely and said, 'Are you badly affected?' (She probably thought I was consumptive.) 'I've had pleurisy,' I replied, 'but I'm better now and I've just come for a change of air.'

She took me to the women's ward and showed me to a bed between two patients with open, running sores; there was a cradle for my baby next to the bed, covered with a piece of gauze by way of mosquito net. I was told to apply to Sister Chantal for the regulation dress: a blue overall with white stripes and the gingham headscarf with red and white checks.

I told Sister Chantal that I'd rather die than stay at the hospital in between two patients with chancres and have to wear hospital clothes. 'I thought that as a former protégée of the nuns, I had a right to more consideration,' I said. She simply replied, 'I knew you wouldn't agree to stay under these conditions, and I told the Mother Superior so.'

So I went back to Michelet. Our friend Habtiche welcomed me back with these words, 'You can make yourself at home in our house for as long as you want!'

And we stayed there till 18 August, forty days altogether! As long as I live, I shall always be infinitely grateful to this man who received us so royally.

Henri had enteritis from the bad milk. Our friend called the doctor who prescribed lactic acid. The child was starved for twenty-four hours. The second evening he was a little better and I gave him the breast again but his mouth and tongue were covered with white blisters; I had to rub them with honey on a rough cloth: he bit my fingers and I despaired of saving him. Finally his mouth got better and he could take the breast again. Then the child's ears started discharging pus which ran down his cheeks everytime I laid him on his side. He had put on weight but the pus formed sores on both sides of his face. The doctor assured me that this was nature's way of getting rid of the poison. Henri was now crawling all over the house and eating any raw tomatoes that he found within reach. I myself was feeling better, the change of air and environment had done me good. Our friend's little girls said in their prayers, 'Jesus, make Henri better!'

I was sufficiently recovered. My mother had been to see me and spent a few days with me in Michelet. My brother came running too and brought me some water-melons to take back to Ighil-Ali. My husband hired a cart, we thanked our hosts for their hospitality and set off back home.

I went upstairs to my room. Many things that I had left there had disappeared, including my shoes, but who could I complain to in that house full of people?

The fig season was drawing to a close and my mother-in-law had put a quantity to dry for the winter. Reskia didn't want to go back to her husband, so she and her mother, Lla Djohra, were once more living with me. My old friend Lalla Aïni, the mother of Lla Djohra, Uncle Hemma and poor Khaled, no longer moved from her bed of sorrow and her eyes could no longer make anything out, but she still clung on to life. Whenever I could find some little delicacy for her, I hurried over with it.

Winter had returned. In the absence of my father-in-law, Ahmed-ou-Amrouche, my mother-in-law went to collect the loads of olives which we put to dry, to have a stock of oil; we had started working on the wool again, for the market, and had a *burnouse* on the loom. Christmas came and New Year's Day. It was 1905. Paul was now at school, in his father's class. Henri was two, he was the most beautiful child in the village. And when the women had an argument, the one would say to the other, 'D'you think you've given birth to Achour-ou-Amrouche, to be so stuck-up?' The whole family loved him and everyone spoilt him.

In February a distant relative died from uremia. This brought grandfather Hacène down from Tizi-Aïdhel. He was as erect as ever. He led his mule into the courtyard and was greeted by all the women who kissed his hand and his head, then he went up to see Taïdhelt. That year he went the rounds of all his fields. He went to the mill that cousin Rabah looked after and which produced a quantity of flour. He sat by Lalla Aïni's bedside, she was slipping away; he thanked her for all she had given him when he was a needy child. He kissed the old woman's hand and head; she died that same night. In the evening he asked Taïdhelt for clean linen as he always left spotless *gandouras* and *burnouses* with her. He had changed in the large room which was icy cold; the wind blew through every chink and cranny. He rode back to Tizi-Aïdhel the next morning on his mule. When I next saw him, a month later, he was already dead!

When he got home that day, he had to take to his bed, from which he never rose again. Realising that he was close to death, he called his children around him: my father-in-law Ahmed and my husband Belkacem set off. They arrived just in time to be present at his death. And when Belkacem asked him: 'What have you done for me, grandfather?' the old man replied, 'I did more for you than for any of the others: I saw to it that you had an education. The pen that I put in your hand is worth more than all the property on earth.' He died a couple of days later.

He was so respected that the people of Tizi-Aïdhel wished to carry his body on their shoulders. They made a litter and the men of the village bore him in relays, as gently as possible so as not to harm the corpse of the righteous man who had lived for years in their midst.

The news had already reached Ighil-Ali, a servant of the family having been sent on in advance of the funeral procession. At about eight in the morning the entrance gates were opened wide to make way for the litter. All the men entered. A rush mat and a blanket were laid down and the body placed gently on them while we all crowded around. I wept bitterly as I was very fond of grandfather. Two sheep had been slaughtered and all the women in the family rolled *couscous* so that all the men who had come from a distance could eat before setting off again for their village.

The dead man's daughters and daughters-in-law gathered round him, weeping. But in one corner of the huge room, a scene attracted my attention: my father-in-law, Ahmed-ou-Amrouche, was secretly haggling with one of our cousins over the sale of a wallet embroidered with silver thread, while his father was lying dead!

A tomb was built out of bricks and cement, lined at the bottom and sides with tiles: and that evening they laid to rest the man who had worked so hard, who had deprived himself of so much, who had run so many risks – and all for the fortune he had amassesd to be squandered within nine years!

Grandfather died on 5 March 1905. By 1914 the house was sold! I noticed that nobody had really mourned him. As soon as the funeral was over, everyone's greed was unleashed. My mother-in-law confessed her pleasure to me. I learned later how welcome the old man's death was to my father-in-law, who was up to his eyes in debt.

Zahra had gone back to her parents when grandfather had made his son swear to separate from this woman who, according to him, had brought misfortune to the house, even before she became a member of the family: it had not been a good omen when the fine mule Gazelle had fallen down the ravine. The son had promised faithfully to obey and the father had died with his mind at rest. He left a baby son, only two weeks old, who was to have an equal share in the inheritance with my father-in-law and so prevent the latter ruining everything.

A few days after grandfather's death, my father-in-law told Belkacem to give up his job teaching at the mission school, as he had a better proposition to make than only earning fifty francs a month. In spite of my advising him not to do anything rash, my husband let himself be tempted.

That same year my father-in-law brought from Aïth-Djellil a new wife to replace Zahra; she was called Smina or Tajlilith. To put himself in the good books of his sisters and his father's co-wives, he had handed back the management of the house to his sister Fatima. This was ruination! When the olives were brought in that year for crushing, the oil was allowed to leak from the presses by the skinful.

There was a lot of whispering at this time, whose meaning I didn't understand. Tassâdit had remarried, a man who met with her approval; and Reskia herself married Lloussine-ou-Hemouche, a soldier on half pay. The atmosphere in the house was stormy. Tassâdit declared that she was the only one who had the right to mourn Hacène-ou-Amrouche, her father, as she was the only one who had lost all her advantages. Meanwhile, my father-in-law had collected in money that was still owing, paid off his debts and, when the inventory of the estate had been drawn up by the official evaluator, he had 35 to 40,000 francs in investments. He bought a fine black mule and, as additional extravagance, indulged in a high saddle, embroidered with gold and silver, and set off to collect his legacy from his father. One day he decided that Zahra must return, as the wife he'd taken to replace her hadn't satisfied him, although she was pretty.

From the first year I realised that everything was going to the dogs. Hacène-ou-Amrouche's last wife, who had a little girl and a boy, demanded her share of the inheritance, but the little boy died within the year. There remained the daughter, who was a minor. The mother went to law and my father-in-law had to let his young half-sister have all the properties at Tizi-Aïdhel and her share of the liquid cash which was put in trust with the notary.

Then it was the turn of the other sisters, Fatima and Tassâdit, who acted on the advice of the latter's husband. Ahmed had been squandering their savings and they were obliged to come to a mutual agreement. The two women were made joint owners of the old house, one olive grove and a fig plantation.

It was now 1906. There had been a lot of snow and it was very cold. We were living in the storehouse which was now empty. I wonder how we managed to survive that year, as we had no resources. My father-in-law was angry with us as my husband had refused to let him have my children circumcised. Belkacem had complained to the Adminstrator who got the *cadi* to issue an injunction forbidding my father-in-law from interfering with the children. As a result of this defiance he wanted to turn us out of his house.

I was expecting my third child. Jean-El-Mouhouv was born 7 February 1906 during a snowstorm. My pains started in the middle of the night and my mother-in-law went to fetch the midwife, while Douda stayed with me. After the delivery I suffered from severe colic, probably because I had caught cold. Paul went down through the snow to tell the Christian families the news and all the men came with their rifles on their shoulders to salute the birth. A few days previously we had received a letter from our friend Habtiche asking my husband to come and help with the census, so that was why Belkacem was away.

We made out as best we could with what my father-in-law gave us. It was no longer Fatima who kept the key to the stores, but my young brother-in-law, Mohand-Arab, Douda's son, who was fourteen or fifteen and rather temperamental.

My husband had left in March and did not return till May or June.

Paul had had the measles. Henri cried for his father, calling for 'Dada Kaci'. That year, 1906, we lived on the little he'd earned and what we got for the two *burnouses* which Lla Djohra and I had woven as, following a quarrel she and I had had with Zahra, my father-in-law had declared that in future we'd have to shift for ourselves.

At one time Taïdhelt had given my father-in-law 5,000 francs to put down as a deposit on a farm he was thinking of buying for her for 65,000 francs, with the livestock, but when it came to paying out the whole amount, Taïdhelt admitted that she'd nothing left. The deposit was returned and the farm sold to people from our area.

Then Taïdhelt bought cousin Amar's house, just behind ours, for her daughter Fatima and her fatherless children, and she moved in, taking everything she could carry, including empty jars and a hand mill. She hardly ever set foot in our house again.

Days, weeks and months went by. With the 5,000 francs Ahmed-ou-Amrouche got back from the sale of the farm, he bought corn and filled up the large alfalfa jar for the last time.

Grandfather Hacène used to say, 'My money is like a broom; any house it enters will be swept clean.' And, in effect, his property brought no advantage to anyone; it even brought ruin to those who acquired it.

With what was left of the 5,000 francs, Ahmed-ou-Amrouche paid the dowry for a bride for his son Mohand-Arab, a sweet girl from Tazayert, with big blue eyes. There was a fine wedding with a drummer and musicians.

One day in July 1909 my father-in-law went to Bougie on business; on his way back he met a troupe of musicians and borrowed a dancer from them (in our country these women are reputed to be of easy virtue). That's the day when Smina – whom Ahmed had married after Zahra – gave birth to my brother-in-law, Ali; Smina's father and mother had arrived from their village, everyone was gathered round the young mother's bed, the women singing 'The Cry of Joy', the men firing their guns. Suddenly my father-in-law threw open the gate of the courtyard and helped a woman down from his mule. Who could this woman be? was everyone's question. Was she a new wife? Then Da L'Mouloud, Smina's father, murmured, 'I know her, she's a dancer!' and all the women sang louder than ever and this woman began to dance. In our parts of Kabylia, nobody would have dared to bring such a creature into his family, where he had wives and daughters and sons who were already adults. That day there was a tornado, the wind blew so hard and the houses shook so much that they seemed to lean over and touch each other. This was God's anger being unleashed. This dancer's name was Aldjia; she spent the night at Taïdhelt's and the next day my father-in-law set off, with his rifle on his shoulder, to take her back to the musicians who employed her. But that day my mind was made up. We had to get away, to leave before there was total disaster. Already several properties had been mortgaged at thirty per cent and soon the interest owing would exceed the capital. All the corn had been eaten, most of the oil jars had been emptied and the oil sold, the house was a bottomless pit: everyone was just concerned with looking after number one, and the master of the house was the worst of the lot. He spent all his time at the café.

I said to my husband, 'We must get out of here! You must go and look for a job before we are left without a roof over our heads.' My husband held out for a long time: he was afraid of the unknown and wasn't a fighter by nature. Often, when I was preparing the midday or evening meal, in the makeshift kitchen under the stairs, I would catch him gazing at my face with a hopeless look in his eyes. And when I asked him why he was staring at me like that, he would answer, 'So that I can remember your face!'

My heart bled for him, but I felt the need for him to go and earn his living elsewhere, as his father didn't give him a penny. When there was a holiday, such as the Feast of the Sheep, his father made him a present of a silver five franc coin. At that time, five francs could buy a day's provisions. But there were five of us to provide for, and with my mother-in-law, that made six.

On Tuesday 7 August my husband left his father's house for the unknown. He had thought himself to be the heir to a great fortune, but he set off like a pauper, on foot. Taïdhelt had lent me three hundred francs which I gave my husband, and I left with her, as security, my anklet set with coral and enamel, my clasps, two pairs of bracelets and grandfather's rifle that had been given to Belkacem. His train was due to leave at eleven o'clock, but he left the house at five o'clock; I walked with him to the end of the Amrouche's alleyway. He met his father who wished him '*bon voyage*' and added, 'If you don't find a job you can come back here, there will always be a bite to eat for you.' But he didn't give him a centime for his travelling expenses.

I learned later that my husband had wept all the way to the station. He reached Constantine that same evening and a few days later I received a letter from him, telling me that he had found work with the railways, earning thirty-nine sous a day (1.95 francs).

I started spinning and weaving again to make *burnouses*, with my mother-in-law's help. I was up before it was light to settle down at the loom from which I only got up to eat, as Lla Djohra prepared the meals. She was sleeping at her daughter's who had just given birth to a boy. Her co-wife Douda, who was still jealous of Zahra, set her a very unpleasant task. She gave her seven eggs that had had cabalistic signs traced on them by initiates, to take to the tomb of a man who had died in exile and leave them there for seven nights. After that time, she had to bring them back and they would cook them for their husband, Ahmed-ou-Amrouche, so that his heart 'would become like a corpse' to Zahra. But the day my mother-in-law brought back the eggs, her own grandson had convulsions and died a few days later, and she thought that God had punished her for violating the tomb of an exile.

Paul was at school, but he had no shoes. I had woven him a *burnouse*. My mother-in-law and I had made two more that a distant relative had sold at the market for seventy francs. (At that time, the best *burnouse* was worth fifty francs). With the seventy francs, we bought provisions for the winter. We bought twelve measures of corn and six of barley, as Lla Djohra said it was better to mix them. We had got in our stock of onions and ground red pepper. As far as food was concerned, we were more or less prepared, but we had neither clothing nor bedding. So, with the wool left over from the *burnouses*, I decided to weave a large blanket to keep us warm in the winter. My husband had given mine to our friend Habtiche, in gratitude for the three months that he had spent with him, with everything found. The children went to visit our relations, who spoilt them – especially Henri.

On 4 November my husband moved to Tunis. He was now earning ninety francs a month, much better than the sixty francs in Souk-Ahras. He sent me little cloth coats for the children. I sold the ones that didn't fit them.

I remember how Jean looked: he was not quite two; he was very slight, with lovely light-brown, curly hair and he would run about the courtyard barefoot in the snow. Henri had black hair, very white skin and a round baby face, whereas Jean's face was oval. In the evening, when the *fellahs* received their dish of *couscous* with bean soup, they called the children over; they would climb on the good folks' laps, and spoon in hand share their meal with them.

This period of my life was miserable, but I was borne up with the hope that one day my husband would have a job which would allow me at last to leave this house in Ighil-Ali, where I was the butt of petty jealousies and was considered a trator to their religion.

At Christmas I received a letter from Father Justrob informing me of my elder brother's death. Mohand had been to see me the previous summer and had hoped to take back a few litres of oil from us, but I hadn't dared to ask my brother-in-law for any as he would have refused to give it to me. Mohand had left empty-handed, to my great distress. He told me then that he and my brother Lâmara had divided up their properties as Lâmara wanted to raise a loan to leave for France, where many of our people were working in the mines and factories; Mohand himself didn't intend to emigrate. So the two brothers had separated. 'Every man labours for his own children,' Mohand had concluded. The news of his death caused me great grief; wherever I'd lived, he'd come to bring me gifts from my mother for the feast days. When I was at Taddert-ou-Fella, he was the one my mother called upon to fetch me and take me back to school. He was very gentle and rather reserved, but nature had not been kind to him as he was inclined to be sickly. Ever since his adolescence he had suffered from some chronic illness that I had not been aware of. Perhaps if he had been better fed and better dressed Mohand would have made a more striking impression . . .

In January a friend of my husband's came to see us; he arrived from Tunis where he worked for the railways. He was allowed a travel pass for his wife, which I was able to use. Meanwhile, Belkacem's employer had decided that his clerk would better be able to give his mind to his work if he wasn't separated from his family, so he advanced him the money for the journey and about mid-February my husband came to collect us.

Belkacem's employer gave him a trunk in which we packed our few clothes and meagre possessions. He had been given a week's leave. And so we left the country.

III

Exile in Tunis

A Family Transplanted

I had only two days in which to finish all the preparations, and though it was mid-winter, I had to get all the laundry dry that Lla Djohra and I had washed in the river. In the distance I watched the mill turning for the last time. I said all my farewells and we left this house where we had thought to spend the rest of our lives.

I had given Taïdhelt the three hundred francs back, so that she could return the jewellery that I had left with her as security, but she made me a present of one hundred francs for our travelling expenses. We walked down to the station, followed by a mule and a donkey carrying the children and our modest luggage. I had removed all the trinkets from my clasps and given them to Lla Djohra. I also left her wool ready for weaving a blanket and the rest of the provisions. But she did not approve of us leaving.

I shall never forget that nightmare journey, on hard wooden seats, next to Arabs who kept on singing the same tune, over and over again.

We slept over at Constantine at the house of one of Taïdhelt's friends, whose son was a policeman. The next day we had to leave for an unknown city. Whether out of ignorance or lack of foresight, I'm not sure, we took with us a distant relative who had neither work nor training. He stayed with us for nearly three months, getting free board and lodging, and left without saying goodbye!

After travelling for a whole day and half the night, we finally reached Tunis. At the station we were met by friends from home: Lloussine-ou-Boubachi and his cousin picked up our luggage between them and took us to our lodgings. Lloussine had ordered a meal from a cheap restaurant, but I couldn't touch anything. They had bought us a horsehair mattress which had been put down on the *seda*, a sort of alcove in the form of a very high bed. There, as soon as we had unpacked the blankets, we all went to sleep. We had arrived at midnight and an hour later, we were in bed.

It was broad daylight when we awoke. I explored the Arab house that my husband had rented for six months. It consisted of two reasonable sized rooms, much longer than they were wide. There was a *seda* in each one, to be used as a bed. There was a third much smaller room from which a staircase led up to the roof, where there was a minute laundry-room. The house had a number of useful shelves; a brick bench in the tiny courtyard had to be used for cooking on, and next to one of the rooms, at waist level, there was the opening to the well. The toilets were at the end of a shed without a door.

We were right in the middle of the Muslim quarter and I didn't speak a word of Arabic. My husband made some essential purchases that same day: a rope and a small barrel for drawing water from the well, some kitchen utensils and a bucket for fetching water from the tap, as the well water wasn't fit for drinking.

The next day Belkacem went back to his office. Paul, a child of seven and a half, had to go to buy the bread, vegetables, coffee and sugar, and fetch water from the tap which was a few yards from the house. Fortunately everything was quite close by. Sometimes, Henri who was four and a half, tried to help his brother carry the bucket, or else a biggish boy brought it as far as our door and I took it inside. I would have made myself too conspicuous if I had gone out, with my face uncovered, amongst all those veiled Muslim women.

I felt very lost, not knowing a word of the local language, Arabic. A neighbour made me understand by signs that she sold charcoal for two sous a kilo and I bought some. No one can ever have any idea of my misery at that period of my exile; when the children were at school and my husband at the office and Jean was asleep, I would go up on to the roof, which faced the avenue, to listen avidly to the language of the Moroccan Chleuhs, which was very similar to the language of my own country! My husband's employer came to visit us, bringing his wife; she gave me a skirt and blouse and invited me to go and visit her at her home in the rue d'Algérie. One day, Henri got lost. He had gone out of the house and walked down Bab-Djedid Avenue. My husband called the police: the child was found in the rue de la Casbah; someone had realised that he was not a local child and had brought him back.

My husband's employer had advised us to send the children to the Lay Brothers' school in the rue d'Algérie. But first they had to have the right clothes. We bought them little suits at a discount and I made them check overalls. I was very scared as they had to cross the rue Algésiras, where the trams ran. Before going off to school Paul did the day's shopping for me at the El-Asser Souk.

When the six months lease was up, I told my husband that the best thing would be for us to go to live in the European district, so that I could go out like the other women. He rented a little flat in the rue Sidi-el-Mordjani, right in the Italo-Sicilian district. With the modest sum at our disposal, we hadn't much choice. This ground-floor flat had only two tiny rooms, a square one which we used as a dining-room and another room that took two beds and our trunk in the corner. A street porter carried all our belongings on his back and we took a cart to ride to our new home.

The Sunday after we moved, my husband went to the auction rooms and bought a sideboard and two beds, one for us and the other for the children. There was nothing to worry about: I had running water in the little kitchen and a flush lavatory that didn't risk getting stopped up like the one in the Arab house.

There were two other families living on the ground floor, opening off the patio; there were three others on the first floor, but one of these was going back to Italy, so their accommodation would soon be free. It was not so damp as ours downstairs, so I decided to take it. My Italian neighbours were very kind to me. I went with them to the Souk to do my shopping. I bought a trough to do the washing in and some cooking utensils. When I wanted to cut out a garment and didn't know how to set about it, they were always ready to help me. Their husbands were workmen, bricklayers, but they were hardworking and thrifty.

In December I had another little boy. The Nuns of Saint Vincent de Paul, who had taken an interest in us, brought me a layette. The boss's wife gave me a pair of linen sheets and a dozen nappies for the baby.

We were as poor as church mice. At the beginning of December, my husband, who disliked writing, sat down every evening to compose New Year greetings for all the people we knew who were likely to send us a little gift. For example, he wrote to the godfathers and godmothers of Henri and Jean, who lived at Saint-Dizier, and to Fathers Baldit, Justrob, Giraud and Dehuisserre. And we waited impatiently for answers to these letters, hoping they would contain a modest postal order. Abbé Godard, Henri's and Jean's godfather, was a great help to us. Many a time he came to our rescue with a hundred-franc note, after we left Ighil-Ali.

Belkacem's employer and his wife were godfather and godmother to the new baby, who we called Louis-Marie. One day, Father Justrob brought me a bag of artichokes and invited me to go to spend Easter Day in Boukris, with the children. He suggested that we go to the mission in Carthage every Sunday, so that the children could have a good meal at his expense. At that time, when life was so difficult, the missionaries in Carthage were very helpful. The children nicknamed the Burser 'Father Lollipop'.

My husband's employer was the agent for several blocks of flats. When one flat fell empty, he offered it to us at the same rental as that paid by the former tenant. In July we moved into this new flat, which comprised a big kitchen, a very long, narrow room which could take a bed, a table and a few chairs, and another square room of quite good size.

This flat was on the first floor, overlooking the narrow, bustling rue Chaker. Every evening there was the sound of Italians singing their serenades, accompanied on their mandolines and on Saturdays they organised parties on the patios, singing and dancing and eating their bean stews. Some of my neighbours spoke a little French and we always managed to make ourselves understood, but I was careful never to ask them for anything, not even a match. These people lived very simply. The women kneaded enormous loaves out of semolina and baked them in the oven; then they wrapped them in cloth to keep them moist. Their midday meal always consisted of macaroni with tomato sauce, and in the evening they would put one of these big loaves on the table and everyone would cut off as much as they wanted, helping the bread down with a mixed salad, tunny fish or cheese. There was never a shortage of wine.

In August I got jaundice and the doctor said I had to go to hospital. I couldn't swallow anything and I was too weak to stand. The Welfare wouldn't look after my children, as we weren't French. Still, I went to the hospital. I pleaded with them till they took me in. My nine-month-old baby was crawling all round the bench where I was waiting, and I thought they would let him stay with me, but the Sister took him to another ward, and to stop him moving around in his cot, she tied both his hands to the bars. I wrote to the nuns in Carthage, asking them to come to my rescue. They took the baby, as well as his brothers who'd been left at home. The girl who the nuns in Carthage put in charge of little Louis-Marie, told me later that he had sores on both his wrists from being tied up.

I remained in hospital from 17 August till the beginning of October 1909, but I was not in time to save my child. One week after I left hospital, he died from an infective enteritis. I've never been able to forget his death, for which I felt myself responsible. *Mektoub!*

I could not bear to live in the rue Chaker flat any longer: I could see my child everywhere, following me around in his little wicker baby-walker. I wanted to find another place. In the same street, in the impasse de l'Eventail, there was a big room with one window over-looking a glassed-in patio; I took it while waiting to find something better, and we moved house again.

We lived in this room, which was quite spacious, from October to December. In December the next-door neighbour gave up his flat: two sizable, square interleading rooms, with two windows overlook-ing the street. There was no door between the two rooms but I bought some cheap material to make curtains, and I put up shelves to keep things off the floor. We slept in one room and the children in the other.

During my illness, one of the chief clerks for the Railway Company had dropped in at the agency where my husband worked. Finding him alone, he suggested that Belkacem apply for a job with the railways. But he would need a medical certificate. Belkacem went for the medical examination. He was afraid he might fail because of his sight, as he had lost one eye from smallpox. But it turned out that the good eye had compensated by developing the strength of both, and my husband was accepted. On 9 December 1909, he began work for the railways.

Before my husband left his first employer, he asked the Fathers in Carthage for their advice. They were unanimous in encouraging him to leave. And Father Justrob, who had been to see his boss, added, 'If you stay on working for him, you'll end up registering as a pauper!'

I never saw this employer again. He had wanted me to work for his wife as a maid, and expected to pay my husband and me a combined wage of one hundred and twenty francs a month. And one morning, when Belkacem's watch was five minutes slow, he was told when he arrived at the office, 'Remember there's a fixed time for starting work, but there's no fixed time for leaving the office!' Sometimes, when there was urgent work, my husband spent part of the night finishing it, but he was never given an hour's overtime pay. His employer refused to pay him for the last month's work. But Father Vincent made it up to us, saying, 'Let him keep it, he won't get rich on that!'

From now on, my husband earned one hundred and twenty francs a month instead of one hundred, and we had other benefits as well as travel passes: we had free medical attention and medicines; we could buy paraffin and soap at cost price. But what delighted us the most was the possibility of at last returning occasionally to our own country, as, without the passes, we would never have been able to save enough to pay for our fares.

The children were still attending the Marist Fathers' school; they'd heard that my husband had left his former employer who had washed his hands of us. As the children were not paying, the deputy headmaster came to see me one day to tell me I wasn't to send them to school any more. (I learned later that only the children from well-to-do families were admitted to this school). So then I decided to go and stay for a few months in Ighil-Ali, as I was very run-down. My husband asked for the travel pass and we left on 12 May 1910. We did the journey in one go, without stopping over in Constantine.

We were still dressed in Kabyle costume; the children wore little white *gandouras* and little *burnouses* made of blue cloth. Belkacem had bought himself a local outfit: the *seroual* (baggy trousers, worn in North Africa), *gandoura* and *burnouse*, with silk sash.

Jean had run a temperature during the journey and when we got to Ighil-Ali I had to put him straight to bed: he had the measles. In Tunis it had been almost summer, but there, in our mountains, it was cold and fires were still being lit. I made myself at home again in the empty storehouse. My father-in-law was still surrounded by his four wives, the last two of which were expecting. One baby was born within a few days of our arrival, the other a month later, both boys: Smina-Tajlilith's son was called Mahmoud, and Zahra's was given the name of Hacène, after the grandfather. I learned that one of the big properties, planted with olive trees, had been sold; and that my young brother-in-law, Mohand-Arab, had repudiated his blue-eyed wife and was now engaged to Zahra's younger sister (Zahra being his father's wife) and that the wedding would soon take place. The two last fields had been mortgaged to pay the dowry and the wedding expenses. Ruin was now complete.

My husband didn't stay with us very long, as he only had a fortnight's leave.

In June there was a terrible storm, it rained for days on end and the river was so swollen that the mill-race could drive the wheel again. A herd of goats was drowned. I had bought a sack of corn and it was a good opportunity to have it ground. They told me that the previous year, in 1909, there had been a typhus epidemic and several families had been decimated.

Belkacem's maternal grandfather had died of old age. Taïdhelt was still at Amar's: she had been struck with the dread disease and had lain in a coma for days. During that time, her son and daughter scraped the bottom of grandfather Hacène's coffers.

Henri had the measles after Jean. Thanks to the cold I didn't have any difficulty in keeping them indoors. Paul was boarding with the Fathers. I asked the mission to grant us a plot of land so that we could build a house, in case of need. Father Dehuisserre promised to let me have one, on condition that I left a right of way between us and our neighbour. I accepted and wrote to tell my husband.

*

One or two nights before my departure, I had a dream. I was standing at the door of the vestibule, looking out on to the courtyard. I looked up and saw countless ropes stretched in all directions across the courtyard, and on these ropes meat hung to dry. An infinite quantity of meat! The sun turned this meat to gold and I said to myself, 'I shall not be there to enjoy any of it, as I'm leaving.' Suddenly a woman appeared at my side, a woman I didn't know, who I'd never seen before. She put her hand on my shoulder and said, 'Does that upset you?' – 'Yes,' I replied. 'Close your eyes,' she ordered, and I obeyed, putting my hand over my eyes. 'Open them now!' And I opened my eyes. All that wealth that had so struck me, had disappeared. 'You see,' she said, 'there'll be nothing left of it all.' Just as I never forgot the dream I had had at Mekla, where the bird of destiny had deposited me opposite the hospital, so I could not forget this dream just before I left this house which was still well-stocked and containing so many resources.

I spent the whole holiday in the house of my husband's family. I gave birth there to my son Louis-Mohand-Seghir. (As the baby who had died in Tunis was called Louis-Marie, I wanted to give the next child the same Christian name.) I saw some of the old women that I used to write letters for, to their children in the city. They told me how much they missed me, as my letters brought them luck.

I came back to Tunis at the end of October. Louis was nearly six weeks old. My house in the impasse de l'Eventail had been white-washed, and I resumed my place among all the neighbours who were pleased to see me back. I was not a nuisance to anyone and I was always ready to do them a good turn.

Marie-Louise, my school-friend from Taddert-ou-Fella, was in service in Tunis; she came to see me occasionally. She had asked if she could be godmother to my latest son. She brought me some nappies and a christening robe. The baby was baptised in Carthage. On 1 January 1911, my husband went alone to Carthage to wish the Fathers a happy New Year. He still wrote his letters every year with our New Year greetings, and on this occasion we did receive some money. Father Dehuisserre slipped a twenty-franc note into his letter, Father Baldit sent a money order for fifteen francs and the godfathers and godmothers in Saint-Dizier sent some linen and a little money. We were able to buy little suits and capes for Henri and Jean, who went to a nearby school, in the rue de l'Eglise.

But one day we received a letter from Father Boquel, the Burser at the Ighil-Ali mission, where we had left Paul as a boarder. He asked us to come and fetch our son: as his father was now earning a good salary, he didn't need the missionaries' charity. He added that we ought to see about building on the plot the mission had granted us, as the ground was getting eroded and, if we couldn't or wouldn't build on it, he would give it to others who were living in the area and whose need was more urgent. My husband asked for a week's leave and went to fetch his son.

When he returned, he brought his mother, Lla Djohra, with him, as well as Paul, as she had quarrelled with Zahra. This new burden made my life very difficult, as my husband earned very little and family allowances were unheard-of. We just had to manage somehow. When I put my mother-in-law's clothes out to wash, with my pile of laundry, my Italian neighbours pointed out that they were crawling with lice. I had to boil these clothes and made Lla Djohra put on everything clean.

From that day I started to look for another place to live; I couldn't stay there, what with the lack of space, and the Italian women looking down their noses at us. After much searching I managed to find a house that was large but had no windows, only two glazed doors, each opening on to a street. You could go in from one street and out by the other; when the door was shut there was no ventilation. There were three good-sized rooms, one of which was completely dark, and a kitchen lit by a skylight. This house was very inconvenient. Nevertheless, I preferred to leave the impasse, where we'd always been too cramped and where we'd had no privacy. I was always afraid of people laughing at me.

We'd only been a month in this new house when there was a theft, and I never found out who was responsible. A friend of my husband had asked me to look after some money for him and I'd put it on top of the sideboard (it was impossible for a child to reach it). And then, when this man came to ask for it back, it had disappeared.

I climbed on a chair and searched everywhere, asking the children, my mother-in-law and her nephew, Rabir, who was living with us at the time, without being able to discover who the thief was. Besides, I learned that a man had died suddenly in the room I was sleeping in, so I couldn't bear to go on living in this house. In addition, we could hear all the noises from the neighbouring house.

Then I found a flat in the rue des Marchands d'Huile. It was on the second floor and consisted of two nice, airy rooms, plus another small one, and a large kitchen and an enclosed balcony whose windows could open, folding back on each other. It was very light; there was a large paved roof where washing could be hung out to dry. There was only one Italian family on the floor below and there was no one at home all day, except the old aunt who looked after the house and prepared the meals; the others were out at their furniture shop.

This place had only one defect: it was beyond our means. The rent was thirty-three francs a month, out of a budget of a hundred and sixty-two francs. We took it all the same, as cousin Rabir offered to pay us a small amount if we let him sleep in the same room as Lla Djohra and the children. But he didn't stay very long – scarcely a month. One day he told me he'd found a handbag at the station, containing money and some jewellery. With this money he hoped to be able to start trading. He applied for a peddlar's licence and left.

It was now 1911, the year when the plan to run a tramway through a Muslim cemetery triggered off the first Arab revolt of the Protectorate period. It was also the year of the cholera epidemic, which raged throughout the summer: my mother-in-law adored fruit, especially melons and prickly pears. Our street was quite near the souk, where they sold fruit, vegetables, meat and materials. That's where I did my shopping. Dressed in a sort of overall, like the Italian women, I could come and go without fear in this Jewish and Italian district.

The children attended the school in the rue de l'Eglise, close by, and in the evenings we could go up on to the roof and breath the sea air; from the window of my room, I could see a great distance, as far as the Belvedere.

The family who lived on the floor below us moved out and some of our country-folk moved in. Like my mother-in-law, they were Muslims and considered us as *M'tournis* (turncoats), but their son, who worked for the railways, was a convert, like us.

Our neighbour, Ali-ou-Bali, was going to Kabylia and Lla Djohra wanted to go with him. For once, we tried to do a little trading: we knew that dried pimentos were an exorbitant price in Ighil-Ali, whereas you could get them for a hundred and twenty francs a hundredweight in Tunis. We thought my mother-in-law would have no trouble in selling this hundredweight of pimentos and making sufficient money to cover her fare. My husband went to Carthage where Father Vincent, my son Louis' godfather, advanced him the necessary money. My mother-in-law foolishly left the lot at Chlili's shop, where I found them still lying when I went back on holiday in 1912.

When she returned to Tunis, my mother-in-law brought her daughter Reskia back with her; Reskia stayed a couple of months with us, then my husband took her back home. While he was there, he visited every member of his family and came back worn out.

1912 had begun; the children had gone with their father to Carthage and come home with pennies, pots of preserves and chocolate. Jean was still a sickly child, he had a poor appetite and didn't like his grandmother's cooking. Henri and Paul were more robust. Louis was a little colossus, but he'd had several attacks of convulsions. So, when the long summer holidays came round, I decided to take him, with his brothers, on a pilgrimage to Our Lady of Africa. I had to pass through Tizi-Ouzou and stop in Tizi-Hibel, to see my mother whom I'd not seen for eight years.

We set off at the beginning of July. We'd written to my father-in-law, asking him to meet us at Beni-Mansour. He turned up as arranged. We continued our journey. In Palestro, we called on Habtiche. He now had a large family, four little girls and two boys and his wife was expecting another baby. Our friend still had the same big, intelligent eyes, with a mischievous gleam, that made you forget his hunchback. He had a fine house, standing in a garden.

From Palestro, we went on to Maison-Carrée, where we were staying with Marie-Paule, who had been at Tagmount; her godfather, Father Bartholomew, was there too and he paid for our board and lodging. Marie-Paule had just had a little boy, her home was very small; she gave us her own bed and made us a good meal. The next day I climbed up to the sanctuary. I noticed women walking barefoot. I attended mass and prayed fervently to the Holy Virgin to cure my little Louis. I was given a blue girdle with big tassels. We spent one more night with Marie-Paule and then caught the train again.

When we got to the station at Tizi-Ouzou, it was midday, and the sun was blazing. We suddenly heard a shout, 'Belkacem-ou-Amrouche!' A man who had been sent to meet us was holding two mules by the bridle.

We had lunch at the miserable station restaurant, and I gave my food to the mule-driver, as it was too greasy for me. When the heat had subsided a little we set off for my village.

We arrived just as it was getting dark; as soon as my mother caught sight of me, she came up and embraced me, saying, *'Dekhem!'* (Is it really you!) and I replied, 'It is indeed me.' I found her greatly changed, she had grown very thin and her eyelids seemed all puckered up; she must have wept a great deal. I hadn't seen her since 1904, in Michelet. My brother Lâmara was in France, as were all the young men from the village. Only women, old men and children were left. I asked mother how my elder brother Mohand had died, she told me he hadn't had a long illness but had gradually faded away, without suffering: he'd left two children, aged eight and four. My mother looked after them as they were from different marriages and their mothers had remarried. My mother couldn't weave large pieces any more, but I noticed she had made little rugs with the wool from her sheep and lambs. She told me the *sheikh* who she'd had so much respect for had died of grief after two of his sons had been killed on their way to Michelet. The murderer was never discovered. His other son, Sidi Sâadi had taken his place, and was as good to my mother as his father had been. She also told me that Lâmara's family and Mohand's children had sold their house to buy a bigger one, where they were all living now, but this had got them into debt. My brother Lâmara had earned enough money in France to pay off his share, but that of the orphans was still outstanding. The *sheikh*, acting for the dead father, advanced the money owed by the orphans, without accepting any interest. As the oil yield had been good, my mother had two full jars which she intended to sell as soon as the price had risen sufficiently. Then she would pay off the children's share. We talked for a long time; she told me how sorry she was not to have been able to find me a husband in the village, as she would then have been able to see me more frequently, and when I replied that everything was for the best, she said that she was the one who had suffered the most from the drama of my birth, as she had been cut off from her family for ever. As for the infamous Kaci, God had given him two sons, and his wife sang their praises as she put them to sleep: God had pardoned the wrong my father had done.

In spite of tiring easily, she still went every morning to fill the water jars for the mosques; I must have stayed from Thursday till Monday. On Sunday I attended mass at the convent. There I met a girl who had been with the nuns at Ouadhias and whose husband had left her; she was living in Tagmount-ou-Kherouche with her brother. That was the village where Alice's father (my school-friend from Taddert-ou-Fella) was the local policeman. I enquired about my friend from this girl. She told me that Alice had refused to go with the Masselot family to Sétif, where the former Adminstrator had been appointed Deputy Prefect. She had married an illiterate Kabyle and worked like the village women. I was very fond of this gentle girl and was sorry to see her end up like this. Marie-Paule, in Maison-Carrée, had told me that Dahbia-Marie was in service with Mme Delfau. That was the last news I ever had of my childhood friends. The year before, Father Bartholomew had told me of Mme Achab's death.

My mother would dearly have liked to keep me longer, but I reminded her that my other children were all alone at Ighil-Ali. She wept bitterly as she embraced me. I never saw her again.

We returned via Tizi-Ouzou. When we reached Allaghan the heat was at its height and I was ill from exhaustion. After trying everywhere to find a lemon, we finally got one from the stationmaster. I was so thirsty that my tongue was sticking to my palate. Mules took us on to Ighil-Ali, where we arrived at four in the afternoon.

I settled in once more in the empty storehouse. I noticed some things had changed: my brother-in-law Mohand-Arab and his young wife weren't there any more. Douda herself was at her parents' and my father-in-law Ahmed-ou-Amrouche had rented the café in Bouza (it was this business that was his final ruin, when he lost everything, including the family home).

We got the foundations dug on the site that the Fathers had given us, to avoid the danger of landslides, or having the land taken away from us. To pay for this, I sold my jewellery, my *khelkhal*, clasps and two pairs of bracelets, all in solid silver; I got three hundred francs for them. The bricklayers built the retaining wall on the road and were able to put up a portion of wall on each side, to mark out the boundaries of the house.

The peppers that I had given to my mother-in-law, for her to sell at a profit for me, were still in Chlili's shop, where nobody had bothered with them. I let cousin Amar have them at the price I had paid for them. Those were the last holidays I spent in the Amrouche house.

Father Ingelet was recruiting pupils for a new school he wanted to start in Aïth-Yenni and talked of taking Paul with him. I refused at first, after the Ighil-Ali experience, but he was so insistent that I wrote to ask my husband's advice. When Belkacem agreed, I bought wool to weave Paul a *burnouse*, as it is very cold in Greater Kabylia. Louis had no more convulsions, but he was very grouchy. I was expecting another child. Henri and Jean played with the other boys from the village, stalking cats and dogs; Jean was only six, he spent a lot of time with me.

Many quarrels broke out between my father-in-law's two young co-wives; it amused me to listen to them. There was also a scene between my father-in-law and his favourite, Zahra: she had given him a fine woollen rug to take to the café and he had pawned it. Everything that could be sold from the house had been sold, even the tools: the large carved chest, the saddle embroidered with silver and gold, the superb black mule, the carpet of thick wool pile, everything, everything had been liquidated. The plantation of prickly pears had also been sold for next to nothing. The only thing left was the roof over our heads. He was in arrears with the rent for the coffee-house, he owed for the sugar and coffee that the customers consumed in this business that precipitated his ruin. Taïdhelt, for her part, went in for ways of making money that were not above suspicion. Many women from the village had left goods with her for safekeeping: widows who wanted to keep something from their deceased husband's house, gave such things to her to look after. A family whose son had gone bankrupt, asked her to store all the goods they had been able to save from the disaster. Her daughter, Fatima, would go to the homes of well-to-do people and fill up goatskins with oil, saying it was water she was taking.

All these wretched women were robbed: they didn't get a penny back, and the family that had left the goods in store had to bring a lawsuit. I learned later that Taïdhelt had given her grandson Dahi enough money to set up in business and she'd bought her daughter and granddaughter silver jewellery, which they kept.

We returned to Tunis at the end of September for the start of the school year, having left Paul as a boarder at Aïth-Yenni. The days passed. Life for me was more difficult than ever: my mother-in-law had been with us for a year, she had her habits that had to be respected. Whenever I or the children had even the slightest quarrel with her, she waited till her son Belkacem came home and then started to sulk; she would go and sit sullenly in a corner. Then Belkacem would say, 'Someone has upset my mother!' And he'd go back to work without eating his lunch. I was so afraid he'd make himself ill! I took Lla Djohra on one side and tried to reason with her. 'You've only got your son,' I said, 'and he's all I've got, so why do you worry him like this? He's gone off without eating again. If something happens to him, you'll be punished as much as me!' But she'd never listen to me, so I had to make an effort never to cross her, so that her son wouldn't be torn between his mother and myself.

We had a number of Kabyle visitors, everyone who came to look for work in the city came to our house first. Among the relatives, there was Bouzid, Saïd and Mohand-Arab, with others who were not even related to us.

We were still living in the rue des Marchands d'Huile through the school year 1912-13. Henri and Jean were still attending the school in the rue de l'Eglise, they played with the Sicilian children and Jean could speak their language as well as they did.

One day, a neighbour from the rue Chaker came to see me. She said, 'Madame Amrouche, why don't you register your children with the Welfare? They get shoes and toys on feast days; I'm going to register mine, would you like to come with me?' So I went along. We waited our turn. Finally we were registered. A little while later there was a distribution of toys, and Mme Christaud and I went along. All I brought back was a tambourine. I had wasted a whole afternoon and carted my son along for such a trifle. At Christmas the children were given shoes with cardboard soles that they never wore. That was the first and last time I ever asked for anything.

At that time I didn't have a sewing machine and I made the whole layette for the baby I was expecting by hand. The Souks were full of all sorts of material, but I chose the cheapest. Louis was still peevish, he was still a baby and I had to carry him everywhere on my back. Jean was thin and fussy about his food; Henri was the only one who seemed healthy enough, but even he was often poorly: probably the house was not well ventilated and the food unsatisfactory, as my mother-in-law had declared that the French bread wasn't filling, so we bought semolina and made bread or *galettes* at home. The children didn't like this but we couldn't afford two lots of cooking.

My daughter Marie-Louise-Taos was born on 4 March 1913, she was the only girl among five boys. The children went off to school and my husband went to the office. Back home, in Ighil-Ali, our neighbour Chlili supervised the work on the house. The surrounding wall had swallowed up a lot of money, but the work went on in spite of the difficulties.

Paul passed his primary-school certificate. We went to Kabylia for the holidays. We occupied our new house although it was not yet finished. The floor-tiles had not been laid and the doors had to be remade, as they were too low. But we had a place to stay; the Kabyle Centre, a society founded the previous year by Father Baldit, had advanced us the money, to be repaid over ten years.

I took one of the downstairs bedrooms and my mother-in-law took the other, with her daughter Reskia. I won't dwell on what those holidays were like, when I couldn't please anyone, neither my mother-in-law nor her daugher, neither her family nor my own children, or myself. I lived through them, nevertheless, trying to humour everyone, so that my husband shouldn't be distressed . . . I'd immediately realised that my sister-in-law was tuberculous, she reminded me so much of her sister Ouahchia when she came to live with us in the early days of my marriage, but it would have caused a scene if I'd dared say anything to her mother. My young children and I used the same utensils for eating as the invalid. When the food was prepared, first of all my mother-in-law gave a generous helping to her daughter; she herself, my children and I had to make do with what was left. Sometimes, even, an aunt came and ate and slept with us. Paul was back from Aïth-Yenni and he used to fetch the water and go to the market every Saturday for us. I bought as much wood as I could and I noticed that it used to disappear, everything disappeared: grain, sugar, wood, but I could never catch anyone at it. The holidays were over at last, but Jean had sore eyes, Henri was running a temperature, Louis was still a baby and Marie-Louise-Taos an infant in arms. My mother-in-law refused to return to Tunis with us. She moved into the old family house in the upper village, with her daughter Reskia. I rented out the upper storey of our house in the Christian village to the district road-surveyor, Lespinasse, who occupied it with his three children.

Moving House Again

When we returned to Tunis, we didn't go back to our former house; during my absence my husband had moved into a house he'd rented in the rue Abba. Because of our limited means, he took these premises together with a Kabyle friend, nicknamed Loulou. We each paid half the rent and shared the use of the kitchen and lavatory.

The rooms of this new house opened out on to a pretty patio with marble paving. A vine climbed up one of the walls of this patio. There were balconies on the first floor, from which the other tenants – French people – could overlook us; that didn't bother me, but Loulou, who was a practising Muslim, was shocked.

Thinking that his mother would be returning with us, my husband had laid in a supply of corn. But all alone, as I was, with two sick children, another who was only a toddler and a baby girl, still in the cradle, how was I to see to this corn? Besides which, my brother-in-law, Mohand-Arab, who had come to try to get a job with the railways, was boarding with us.

Jean had to be taken to the occulist, who said his condition was serious: he had to stay at the hospital for two or three days before any decision could be made. The child was only seven. Belkacem had to go to the office. I had the other children to look after as well. And now, someone had to sit with Jean all night and wash out his eyes, to get rid of the pus. A relative agreed to stay at the hospital with him. Jean was only allowed home after three days.

I spent whole nights without sleep, going from Jean to Henri, from Henri to Louis, from Louis to Marie-Louise. When we were in Kabylia, Henri had followed a funeral procession and watched the corpse being laid in the grave, and since then, either from fear or from the excitement, he had been running a temperature every night. We sent for the railway doctor who prescribed some medicines, but we had a long struggle before he was better.

A few days after being discharged from the hospital, Jean was able to open his eyes and eat without help at last, but he had to go back every day to the rue Zarkoun for treatment. One day, I saw him come home with his eyes closed. He'd had drops put in and he said it felt as if he had a thorn in his eye. I lifted up the lid and found a piece of dropper in his eye; the nurse must have had a broken dropper . . . When Jean's eyes were finally better he had a course of injections at the Pasteur Institute. He was not able to go back to school till the end of October. He retained a little mark in his eye, fortunately far from the pupil. Henri and Jean were admitted to the Petit Collège, where the books were free. Paul was attending the Alaoui Collège.

At last I could see to sifting the corn and getting it ground. Loulou's mother-in-law was very kind: she looked after the baby for me while I worked, and Loulou's wife, Djohra, was very fond of Louis who was quite happy to stay with her while I was sifting the corn or preparing the food. The meal had to be ready by eleven o'clock for Mohand-Arab, and by twelve for my husband and the children who came home from school.

*

That year was particularly difficult. Fortunately, my health was not bad. In January we had to give notice to leave the house we'd been living in, as the lavatories were always blocked, with stones stopping up the drains. Loulou and Belkacem discovered a large Moorish-style house in the Bab-Aléoua district, with four nice rooms and an entrance hall. We were to occupy two of the rooms, Loulou another and his mother-in-law the smallest; there remained the entrance hall where Loulou's brother and my brother-in-law, Mohand-Arab, had to sleep.

This house had a huge patio paved with smooth flat stones. We cooked on *kanouns*, inside the house in winter and in the courtyard in the summer. I made large loaves of bread like the Italian women and sent them to be baked in the baker's oven; I prepared Kabyle dishes, noodles, *couscous*, or *bercouquès* (large grains of *couscous*, steamed and dropped directly into the broth).

That year the children went to Carthage without me, for New Year's Day. Ever since my first little Louis was buried, I never went with them again, as I had an aversion to Carthage and from 1909 I never set foot in the convent there again.

We had succeeded in getting naturalised. My husband was contributing to his retirement pension, which was progress; nevertheless, he still kept up the job of writing greeting letters. This was a veritable torture for him, but I couldn't do it for him, as I can't write to strangers, I never know what to say to them . . . It's true he was earning a bit more, but we were a big family. We had to send a little money to the grandmother, who'd stayed behind with her sick daughter, clothe the children, find shoes for them and, most important, we had to eat: my husband was often forced to buy second-hand clothing that I boiled and left for several days and nights lying out in the sun and air before using. Father Julien came to see us, when he was passing through Tunis with Father Manfred who left a little money for the children. Father Vincent had left Carthage, but didn't forget us, although he was far away. Father Baldit, Father Justrob and Father Dehuisserre all helped us to a greater or lesser extent. Brother Georges and in particular Abbé Godard did their best, when we were really in need.

My sister-in-law Reskia died in February 1914, in spite of all her mother's care. Her little girl had died before her. Reskia had told her broken-hearted mother, 'I am glad that my child has died before me. How would you have been able to look after her?' Lla Djohra waited impatiently for us to return to Ighil-Ali for the holidays. As soon as school ended, we set off, only stopping over for one night at Souk-Ahras, where we slept at Cousin Mouhou's (the nickname of Mohand-Amoqrane).

My husband had applied for a post as primary school teacher in Morocco. The Fathers had found posts for several Christians, but man proposes and God disposes. Just when it was least expected, 2 August, war broke out, and I had to spend the rest of the year in Kabylia, as Belkacem could be called up at any moment: he was only thirty-two.

My father-in-law had repudiated all his wives except Zahra, who had said to the others, 'You can all go, there'll always be enough left for me!' But there was nothing left, Ahmed had had to sell up the café in which he had sunk the last remnants of his father's fortune. Now he had to work as a *fellah* for other people, he was the one who had to thrash the olive trees. When his house was put on the market, he said to me, 'Sell your house and you can buy mine!' 'And what should I do with your house?' I retorted. 'Buy it so that the children of your sisters Fatima and Tâssadit can come and foist themselves on me? I've already lost enough, having the upper storey built on the house that you couldn't manage to keep! I'm not throwing good money after bad!' He would come and see me from time to time to ask me for five francs and I always told him I hadn't got it.

In November my husband passed his medical and was taken into the army. He asked for a couple of days leave to come and say goodbye to us before joining his regiment. He left us on 17 November. The next day, his half-sister Hemmama died of exhaustion. So he lost two sisters in the same year.

A few days later I received a letter from Belkacem: he'd been sent back to his job with the railways, as he was the father of five children. I was delighted, and so was Lla Djohra. I had been making the necessary arrangements for spending the winter there: I had bought in stocks of corn, dried beans and figs (figs are very good for children). Marie-Louise-Taos could walk by herself; she used to crawl upstairs to see the road-surveyor, Lespinasse, who was very fond of her.

Lespinasse now only occupied one room on the first floor, as his sons Jean and Charlot were at the front and Marius was studying with the Fathers.

I had bought olives which I'd spread out on the tiled floor, waiting to get them pressed to have a stock of oil. In the spring of 1915 builders came to start work on putting up the school. One of them brought his wife with him and asked me if I'd rent him the room on the first floor, which was empty. I agreed: it meant ten to fifteen francs in hand, which I added to the fifty francs my husband sent me to feed my four children, my mother-in-law and myself, and to buy wood . . . And I often noticed my stores 'evaporating'. More than once I caught my mother-in-law's sister Aldja with provisions that she'd been given by Lla Djohra, who always put her own family first.

The children attended the mission school: Henri was in Father Garisson's class and Paul was taught by Merzoug, a former mission pupil who was now a pupil-teacher in charge of the youngest children. I had had little open shoes made for them, but most often they left them at home and went barefoot, like all the village children.

Hemma, my husband's uncle, was detailed to guard Tirilt-n-Sidi-Ahmed's olives. All the villagers had the right to a plot of ground in this area where they could lay out the olives they'd picked, to let them finish ripening and dry in the sun. Every year, in the olive season, one man was appointed to watch over them. He would build a little *gourbi* (shack) at the side of the road and spend the night there, to see that no one came to steal. He was supposed to be paid in kind when the olives were dry.

Henri and Jean often spent the evening with him. He was a very simple, jolly man, always content with his lot, provided he had his cup of coffee, his snuff and a bit of *galette* or *couscous*. He asked for nothing more. (His nephew Rabir was more shrewd and less honest.) He told the children funny stories and they liked staying with him in the smoky little *gourbi*. Often cousin Chérif-ou-Amrouche, who was fond of Hemma, brought his supper along too, to share with him. Since Hemma had to watch over the olives, the Amrouche family didn't go to spend the evenings in his house as they used to. Previously, in fact, Chérif, Saïd, Seddik, Salah and Madami would chat for hours on end in his house, to the despair of Hemma's sister Mbarka, who complained that she used up all her oil during these long evening sessions. In 1914, many of the Amrouche family were already missing.

Those who were there now arranged to meet in turns in Hemma's hut, to listen to him telling all the *Tales of a Thousand and One Nights*, which he knew by heart. However much I scolded Henri and Jean when they came home in the dark, frozen through, they would return the next day, and that went on all the winter. In the morning I cooked them a big dish of semolina with oil and red pepper to give it a bit of colour, and they ate it up heartily, finishing their breakfast with figs that I bought a measure of every week. They were never left hungry. At midday, I gave them *galette* with fresh olive-oil and figs, or noodles or some Kabyle dish; in the evening, it would be *couscous* with dried or green vegetables, according to what I could get; on Saturdays they always had a little meat.

I had got hold of some black wool to weave a *burnouse* but there was not enough, so I let the nuns have it. I had tried to buy oil to resell when the price was at its peak, but I think I was robbed by Lla Djohra's nephew, as I didn't find the full amount when I wanted to dispose of it and I got nothing for my trouble.

That year spent in Kabylia didn't come up to my expectations. I met with a great deal of jealousy and pettiness. I thought that as we Christian women were all more or less outsiders, we would all stick together, but I only experienced malice, envy, lying, injustice and slander. So I wrote to Belkacem to come and fetch me as soon as possible.

Belkacem arrived during July. I said goodbye to Taïdhelt, whom I'd seen a lot of in the course of the year, and to all the relatives from the upper village, and I left for Tunis with my mother-in-law, my children and my husband. Paul remained behind as a boarder in Manegueleth.

It was yet another lodging that welcomed me, as Belkacem had rented three modest rooms in a small house in the rue du Fossé. I settled in to the one Belkacem was occupying and the children and Lla Djohra had to make do with sharing the two others with Loulou's mother-in-law and Lhossine-ou-Bouchachi's mother, Aldja-t-Kaci, who had arrived before us. We had to put a bed in the courtyard where we took it in turns to sleep as it was the hot season.

The chief clerk in my husband's office suggested to him that I should go to work there, but I wasn't keen. So Belkacem wrote to the Fathers, asking them to send Paul back, as he now had enough education to work as a clerk although he was still quite young: he had just turned fifteen.

He turned up one night without warning and came knocking at our door while we were asleep. And when we called out to know who was knocking, he replied, 'Don't you know Poupoul-ou-Amrouche?' He was starving as he had left his food for the journey behind at Beni-Mansour, in his hurry to catch the train. Two days later, he started work for the railways at Fath-Allah. He got up at five o'clock, came back for lunch and left again at one. His father bought him a suit, so that he was presentable.

At the end of the summer we moved out of the little house, as Lou-lou was no longer living with us. And this time, we rented a big Arab house in the same district, which we shared with Lhossine-ou-Bouchachi: an entrance hall, one very fine room at least twenty-five feet square, plus another for the children. Lhossine had a bedroom for himself and a very small one for his mother. There was a well of brackish water in the large paved patio, and a tank of water that was good for the laundry, but not drinkable.

I was expecting a baby. I was unwell; I had no energy and no appetite. We sent for the doctor who had urine tests done, which showed that I had albuminuria. A few days later I miscarried, and then I recovered. Jean attended the Bab-Aléoua primary school, only a few yards from the house, and Henry, who had passed his primary-school certificate in Ighil-Ali, went to the secondary school, but he was so much behind the other children that the master wondered if he really had obtained the certificate. Although Paul had started work in the office, he still wanted to continue his education. One of his friends named Casanova lent him the lesson notes, from his class. During the day, Paul was earning his living and at night he studied for his secondary-school certificate. I bought a very old general course book, second-hand, in which all the exercises were explained, and I went through them with him. The headmistress of the Bab-Aléoua school corrected his French compositions for him.

*

Paul had been to my village, Tizi-Hibel, to see my mother before returning from Kabylia, and told me that her health was failing. She had said to him, 'O my son, I shall die without seeing your mother again!' Although, with our large family, we were in need ourselves, I sent her ten francs, through the Fathers in Tagmount. A little while later, the money order was returned to Carthage: my mother was dead.

I wept bitterly for my mother as I hadn't seen her since 1912 and I'd not been able to help her at all. I now had no more links with my native village.

The district where we lived was near the railway line and the children, Louis and Marie-Louise-Taos, used to run to meet their father at the level-crossing.

The New Year (1916) had come round and with it the task of writing the greetings letters. The children went with their father to Carthage and 'Father Lollipop' gave them an enormous pot of chestnut purée.

An old engineer had taken an interest in Paul and let him leave work early so that he could attend evening classes at the Brothers' school in the rue de la Casbah.

The Company had opened a Commissariat, where all the employees could buy their provisions; the amount of their purchases was deducted each month from their salaries. The children went for certain foodstuffs, such as pasta, coffee, sugar, semolina. There was not much variety in our food, but no one went hungry.

One day, cousin Bouzid, who was a brakesman, brought us a basketful of dates: a sack had come open in the train and he had filled up his basket. The children had a real feast, but my mother-in-law didn't want to eat up her share all at once. She picked out the best dates and carefully laid them in a blue sugar tin that we had just emptied. We had an infant's high chair that was no longer being used and which I'd hung up in the store-room where Paul slept and worked. Lla Djohra went and hid her tin on top of that chair.

Jean and Henri were each attending their respective schools, Louis and Marie-Louis-Taos were still too small and they stayed at home, playing. The next October, Louis could go to nursery school at last, and the following year Marie-Louise could go too. We were living right in the Arab quarter, among the poor dock-workers. My mother-in-law made friends with some of these women, who would do her a good turn, when she needed it.

One day we received a letter from my father-in-law, Ahmed. He had liquidated everything and wanted to come to Tunis to look for work, so that he could feed his youngest children. In addition, my brother-in-law Mohand-Arab (sometimes called Abbas) was coming home on leave from the front. On 1 July 1916, my husband went to meet them. I've never known such a scorching day in all my life; a violent sirocco was blowing and the sun was blinding: the glare from the whitewashed walls was deadly. God only knows what Belkacem suffered that day: the travellers didn't arrive till midnight.

I found it a bitter pill to swallow: to give hospitality to this father-in-law who had squandered a fortune and now foisted himself on us, when he'd let us leave empty-handed! But I had to bow to the inevitable. My husband said, 'He's my father, so what do you expect me to do?'

Ahmed expected us to find him work, but he was over fifty-five and no one wanted him. At the café he got to know a few Moroccans, who took him on to look after the grapes on a farm. He'd left his wife Zahra and her children with no means of support. He accepted the Moroccans' offer, spent a month and a half in the open, and came back with a few pence. Then, when we had bought him some clothes and his son had got him a travel pass, he decided to return to his family.

There were a great many other railway employees living in Bab-Aléoua. All these families had children attending the same school as Jean. He suffered from chronic toothache, he was very thin, but extremely bright, so much so that he was always top of his class.

In the evenings he played in the large square in front of the school, with all the other children of his age: they played football or hide-and-seek. This district turned out better than the Italo-Sicilian quarter in the rue de l'Eglise – the park in the rue des Moniquettes had a particularly bad reputation.

In May 1916 Paul left the railways and in June he took the school certificate examination, but he failed. I coached him during the holidays. I'd started reading again: Paul brought me books from the Popular Library for which he'd taken out a subscription. I read all the novels by Alexander Dumas the Elder. I was able to help Paul in literature and when he sat the exam again in October he got very good marks (but I wasn't able to help him with science, which I'd never done). He passed this time and was accepted at the teachers' training college.

He started there in October; all his expenses were met: he was given a uniform and shoes, but we had to provide him with bed-linen, shirts, underpants and clothes for everyday wear. Although he was bright, Paul was like me when I was young: he didn't like certain subjects on the syllabus (especially arithmetic and science) but he was always top in French literature.

I'd had to card and spin wool to knit socks for the children and a winter shawl for myself. On 20 December my son Noël-Saâdi was born. The house was chock-a-block. The Ali-ou-Bali family, who'd arrived from Kabylia to join their son who was a stationmaster somewhere or other, had descended on us: there was the father, mother, two daughters-in-law and two small children. We had to put them up and feed them all for two days. They left the morning Noël was born, but not until they'd breakfasted on coffee and bread.

Marie-Louise-Taos and Louis had both had measles, but Louis had got over it completely, whereas Taos had caught cold and suffered from earache. I had to rock her to sleep with a cord tied between her cradle and my bed. She cried all the time, saying over and over again in Kabyle, 'My ear! my ear!'

Noël was a lovely sturdy baby from the very beginning, but a few days after he was born, he began to cry a lot. I sent for the railway doctor and wrote 'Urgent' on the note. When the doctor came, he looked at the child and said, 'D'you think you can make me come any faster, by putting "Urgent"?' From that day, I never once bothered a railway doctor again. When I sent for a doctor, I was able to pay him out of my own pocket. To get back to the baby's illness, I noticed that he stopped crying when his ears were covered; so I came to the conclusion that that was where the trouble was and treated him with warm oil in his ears.

The children went to Carthage again, coming back with pennies and pots of jam. 1917 was the last year that my husband wrote greetings letters. Marie-Louise-Taos' godmother sent us a small amount – forty to sixty francs – and we managed to buy a sofa and a chest of drawers to keep our linen in.

We had the big house in Bab-Aléoua all to ourselves now. Henri and Jean put their bed in the long room that our neighbour had vacated on returning to Kabylia, my mother-in-law shared a room with Marie-Louise, the end room was used to store grain and other provisions – soap, paraffin – and Paul slept there when he came home for the holidays.

None of the children was ever as devoted to his brothers as Paul was. They were more like his children than his brothers: he delighted in buying them little treats. In summer, if he had a few pence, he'd buy them a big melon that he sprinkled with sugar, or sometimes, if he had a bigger amount, he bought thrushes or starlings . . .

I had to punish Paul much more than any of my other children, as he had the knack of making me angry; when he was small and I sent him on errands, instead of hurrying back, he would gamble the money for what he called a 'gilat' (*gelato*, ice cream), and whether he won or lost, he had no idea of the time. Later, he would hire a bike for an hour, and pay for it out of the housekeeping money. That year he was going on seventeen. During the holidays he wanted to go to Port-Gueydon, to see his godfather, Habtiche. I was alone in Tunis with Henri, Jean, Louis, Marie-Louise-Taos and Noël, still in his crib. The war was still on and we had to queue for paraffin and oil. We'd bought two or three sacks of semolina to roll out for *couscous*. Félicité, my school-friend from Taddert-ou-Fella, had caught up with me again after ten years, and came to see me every day with her son Areski. She promised to help me roll the *couscous* and I started the job, but one fine day she didn't turn up and I had to finish the work myself. Jean and Henri helped me as best they could; Henri went to fetch water from the well and Jean did the washing-up and the cooking (he could cook pasta in sauce already and *chekchouka*). I finished rolling out the *couscous*, both the coarse and the fine, and put it to dry on a rush mat covered with a large white sheet.

Paul came back from visiting his godfather in Greater Kabylia with good news: that fine family had had another addition, but Habtiche missed his house in Palestro.

In 1918 my husband fell ill: an intercostal cyst. He had to stay in bed for several days; finally the abscess burst. The Union managed to get us a small raise: the children got an allowance of ten francs a head. We received twelve to thirteen hundred francs in retrospect. I took three hundred of this to buy a little household linen, sheets especially. I bought sheeting and cut out six pairs of small sheets for the children and four big ones for my bed.

We'd picked up a second-hand sewing machine, but some of the parts were very worn. However a Singer representative happened to call and he agreed to take over the machine for the price we'd paid and deliver us a new one, to be paid off in monthly instalments.

About this time my husband had the idea of buying the house in the rue de la Rivière (the street that appears in Marguerite Taos' novel, under the name of rue des Tambourins). All we had was the thousand francs backpay, which we'd put into National Savings Bonds. Lla Djohra had given us her dead daugher Reskia's bracelets and clasps. I hadn't a stitch to put on my back, except for a black and white check overall, but in spite of that we bought the house which was in the hands of a Jewish lawyer named Burgel.

Paul had enlisted in the North African Light Cavalry. He had to get to Oujda (on the border between Algeria and Morocco). He didn't tell us until he'd already signed on. He told us that the war was going badly and that all his age-group would be called up. He at least, so he said, had been able to choose which branch he'd serve in. He'd just turned eighteen and we had no choice but to bow to the inevitable. The evening before he left, he insisted on the children having a real treat: semolina *couscous* with meat and red sauce, like we had in Ighil-Ali. That night neither of us slept. We put down a mat in the courtyard and lay side by side till dawn. Then he got up, washed himself, drank his coffee, kissed all the children, one after the other, kissed his father and grandmother: I was the last. He took a little suitcase with some food for the journey, and he left.

That was the first departure! It was from that day that I started to recall all the poems and songs of exile of my native country. While I nursed my youngest child, I nursed my sorrow, and heavy tears ran down my face. How many songs have I sung since then! How many tears have I shed! I wonder how my eyes can still see clearly, after all the tears I have shed.

We did not take possession of the house in the rue de la Rivière till 1 November 1918, as it was let and the tenant refused to leave. The owner of the house in Bab-Aléoua had in fact given us notice to take effect in the New Year as his son was getting married and he wanted to move back in.

The children, Henri and Jean, went to borrow a little cart that Mme Christaud was kind enough to lend us; and the whole day then went to and fro, transporting as much as possible. I think that we only had to load the beds and the sideboard, as well as the chest of drawers, on to the *araba* (cart) that we'd hired; when it was already dark, my husband and I took a cab with the youngest children and drove off to our own house at last, where no one could ever tell us again that we were a nuisance and would have to leave!

Rue de la Rivière

What delight I felt the next day, when I took possession! At last I owned a house! My children would be in their own home. How many times had I been asked, when looking for lodgings, 'Have you got any children?' And when I answered, 'Yes,' been told, 'We don't let to people with children, they do too much damage.'

Our house had four reasonable-sized rooms, two with windows overlooking the street; a very long dining-room that was lit from the tiny courtyard through a fanlight, and through a glazed partition that led on to the terrace. There was, in addition, an outhouse, a kitchen, a laundry and a coal-shed. It was more than enough for us. Henri and Jean took possession of one of the rooms overlooking the street, I took the other, my mother-in-law, Marie-Louise-Taos and Louis shared the third. In the dining-room, which formed a passage, I put the table, a few chairs, the sofa and the sideboard.

As charcoal was getting scarce, we had a fireplace built in the kitchen so that we could burn wood, since we could get eucalyptus-wood sleepers from the Company. Henri and Jean went to the station with a handcart to collect them. We also had the courtyard paved. Jean was on holiday then and was pleased to help the builder and so earn a few pence.

I hadn't been back to Ighil-Ali since July 1915. I returned in 1919. There were many new graves, and many faces missing in the Amrouche family. Taïdhelt was dead, so were Touêla and her son Salah, and cousin Chérif's wife Sassa. Hemma was the only one left of my mother-in-law's family and he was living with his sister Aldja. This greatly saddened me, it was as if a part of my own existence had vanished with all these people that I'd left in good health. The death of Taïdhelt, grandfather Hacène's wife, grieved me the most; I learned that she had died in great poverty and that she'd been half starved during her last years.

I attended the party that the nuns and their girls arranged for Father Dehuisserre's feast day. I asked for my son Louis to take his first communion here, but they refused on the grounds that he hadn't been instructed in that parish. After three months I was quite glad to leave. The last of my sisters-in-law, Zehoua, had married cousin Bouzid, the brakesman, replacing her sister who had died in 1915 from puerperal fever.

I came back to Tunis at the beginning of the school year. Textbooks and exercise books had to be bought for the children, with four of them now at school, and I didn't get any of their requirements free at this period. The rue de la Rivière neighbourhood was nothing like Bab-Aléoua. It was an Arab district, but much more prosperous, and no dock-workers lived there. It was taken for granted, among these people, that any local woman who went out with her face uncovered, where she could be seen by men, was not respectable. I learned this later. As long as we lived in an Italo-Sicilian neighbourhood, or at Bab-Aléoua, no one took any notice of that: to the Italians I was the

French woman married to an Arab, as my husband firmly refused to give up his fez, even when it stood in the way of his getting promotion (and he was the only one of all his colleagues, even including the chief clerk, who had his school certificate). In Bab-Aléoua we'd been swallowed up among all the other railway employees who were our neighbours. In the rue de la Rivière, it was quite different: our neighbours were all well-to-do Arabs or Kabyles, most of them owning their own homes. The children didn't play in the street, like the ones we'd known till then. All this made quite a change. When Henri went off to the church guild, he was the only one of the Catholic children to wear a fez and he was picked on by the Arab youngsters, who tried to start a fight with him, for associating with *Roumis*. I felt from the beginning that this district didn't suit us, but there we were, and we had to stay and make the best of it. I didn't mention any of this to my husband, but I discovered later that he was aware of it himself. Meanwhile, my old friend Félicité, who lived nearby, came to see me. I also got to know a Kabyle woman, married to a very rich man. She was very advanced as in her youth she had been an artist. She invited me to visit her. Her name was Baya, and she was extremely beautiful.

Marie-Louise-Taos, who had had the Spanish 'flu and been at death's door, was now fully recovered and no longer suffered from earache. She attended the Canton School; a number of little girls came to call for her and they went together. Louis went to the Debarre School and Jean and Henri were at the Alaoui Secondary School.

We still ate Kabyle style and still made huge loaves of bread that we took to be baked in the baker's oven, but Jean disliked certain of his grandmother's dishes that she made very oily and too hot and spicy. Arguments ensued and whenever I could manage I gave Jean a few pence so that he could buy himself something extra. Occasionally, when Lla Djohra had hidden some sweetmeats in her little trunk, shut with a padlock, Jean slid his thin hand under the lid and removed some of her titbits to eat after the meal. Epic scenes ensued. In this way, he had gradually emptied the box of dates which Lla Djohra had hidden away on the high chair in Bab-Aléoua. I remember her coming to confront me in a fury, accusing me of letting my children deprive her of her dessert. I made a show of punishing the offender.

Another time, a friend of the family had brought us some bunches of raisins. There were a lot of them, nearly two kilos. Lla Djohra gave a few to the children and put the rest away in her little trunk. Day after day, Jean slid his thin hand in and drew out a bunch which he slipped in his pocket before setting out for school, and when he came home in the afternoon he took some more to eat at four o'clock. One day his grandmother opened her case to make a *couscous* with raisins: all that remained were a few stalks.

That day, there was a terrible scene: she screamed with rage. I took a stick to punish the culprit but he climbed on to the roof of the outhouse which we used as a lumber-room and coalshed. That was the end of the story. I told my mother-in-law, 'When we have anything special, eat your share with us.' Occasionally, when the children had a penny, she would sell them something that she had hidden: almonds, dates, walnuts, hazelnuts that a friend had given us. For a long time we couldn't afford to buy fruit. The children only saw oranges and mandarines appear on the table at Christmas and New Year. As for other fruit, grapes, figs, apricots or peaches, the season could go by without our ever tasting them, unless we spent our holidays in Kabylia, where there was always a relative or friend to offer us figs or grapes.

I remember one day Paul ventured into a field that didn't belong to us. He brought back a lovely basket of black figs, with a dewy bloom on them, nearly as fine as the ones my mother grew in her field in Tizi-Hibel. When I asked him, 'Who gave them to you?' he replied, 'Lakhdar-ou-Ouakouche'. So I knew he'd been into the field belonging to Yamina-t-Ouakouche, a distant relative who was not particularly friendly. She didn't know Paul by sight, but she asked for him everywhere. When she saw me she said, 'Are you Poupoul-ou-Amrouche's mother?' 'Yes,' I answered. 'He went into my field without my permission; if he'd said, "Lalla Mina, will you give me some figs?" I'd have given him some with pleasure.' I apologised to her profusely.

The house opposite ours in the rue de la Rivière belonged to Kadour-ben-Haroun, a Kabyle from Aïth-Abbès, whose family had left Kabylia in 1871, or even earlier. Only the old people spoke the Kabyle language. My mother-in-law got on well in this environment; as a practising Muslim, she was in her element. To these people I was an unbeliever, as to her I was a woman who'd abandoned her religion and went out with her face uncovered.

In a book by Myriam Harry, *Tunis la Blanche* (White Tunis), I read a description of a Jewish quarter. She spoke of a family in which the grandmother wore the traditional Jewish costume – loose trousers and a pointed bonnet on her head; the mother wore an Italian-style housecoat, while the daughter dressed in the latest Paris fashion. I thought how similar this was to my own family: my mother-in-law draped Arab-style in her blanket, me in my Italian smock and, later, Marie-Louise-Taos in her Paris fashions. I gave up setting foot outside the house, except on rare occasions; besides I had nothing to wear.

Although the armistice of 1918 had been signed, neither Paul nor Belkacem's brother Abbas (Mohand-Arab) had returned. They did not turn up till December 1919, almost simultaneously. My husband had made every effort to keep his brother's job for him in the Company workshops.

I had one sofa and I asked my friend Baya to lend me another one, and Paul and Abbas slept in the dining-room which was very big.

Paul went back to the teacher training college in January 1920 and Abbas went home to fetch his wife and children. When he came back he had with him his cousin Bouzid (who was also his brother-in-law), together with the latter's wife and little daughter. I had to put up all these people one January night and they spent the whole of the next day with us. They left us at last, as Mohand-Arab found two rooms to let in the rue El-Korchani.

When I look back on this period of my life, I wonder how I managed to survive. I had to settle down at the sewing machine to make shirts and also dresses for my little girl. In 1920 Henri passed his school certificate and began work with the railways. Jean passed his school certificate in June 1921 and went on to the training college in October. Paul, meanwhile, had been appointed to the Sfax Primary School. Only Louis, Marie-Louise-Taos and Noël were still at home. Noël was a beautiful baby, full of charm, so beautiful that people turned round to look at him when I held him by the hand. He had a light milky complexion, black curly hair, huge black eyes, with long curled lashes, a straight nose, and a little mouth, red as a cherry. He had a voice like a nightingale when he sang what the called his 'son-songs'. In 1921 I had a severe attack of bronchitis. They sent us word from Kabylia that my father-in-law had injured his knee badly, trying to cut down a tree in his garden in the mountains. My husband and his brother Abbas left. They found their father out of danger, but penniless. They brought back with them the four children from the two different marriages: Zahra's two went to their aunt, we took Smina-Tajlilith's.

I don't know if the question of religion influenced my mother-in-law, but in any dispute, she always found me or my children in the wrong. Whenever a quarrel broke out between the Arab children and mine, she invariably reprimanded my children.

She bought her groceries from Hemida, our neighbour; one day, when I pointed out that he'd made a mistake, she replied, 'It's you who can't count, Hemida doesn't lie, he says his prayers.' What can you reply to that?

As soon as my father-in-law's children arrived from Kabylia, she took them under her protection, alleging that mine ill-treated them. I put up with the situation for a few months and then declared that if this state of affairs continued I would walk out. My husband went to get the Fathers in Carthage to deal with the problem and they sent Ahmed's four youngsters to Kheratta, one of their homes in Kabylia.

Paul left Sfax in May (May was always a fateful month for him). He'd gone back to the army to finish his military service. He stayed there till December. During the holidays Jean took his grandmother, Lla Djohra, and his grandfather's four children back to Ighil-Ali. Henri had been sent to Gaffour by the Company. I was alone, ill, with the youngest children. Paul asked for compassionate leave to come and look after me. He was wonderful. Doctor Broc came to see me and told me I was expecting another baby; I was shattered. I already had a son of twenty-one. And when I said I couldn't believe it, the doctor said, 'You'll see in a month or two!'

Lla Djohra came back from Kabylia. Paul returned to barracks in Forgemol, as I was feeling better. It was very hot and, after supper, we would go for walks outside the town, behind the ramparts, as far as Lake Sedjoumi.

At the beginning of 1922 Paul told us that he was giving up teaching. He asked us for a little capital so that he could open a shop. We gave him the money we'd put aside for finishing the Ighil-Ali house in 1923. We set him up in a grocery business in one of the rooms that opened out on to the street, thinking that this would be a way of keeping him with us. Influenced by his grandmother, he had written to his old school-friend from Ighil-Ali, Louis Ouari, asking him to sound out his father to see if he'd let him marry his daughter Charlotte.* He only told us about this afterwards. As the girl's father and eldest brother agreed to the match, we had no alternative but to give way.

René-Malek, my youngest child, was born on 15 March 1922. Paul wanted to be his godfather. In July we went on holiday to Ighil-Ali, to prepare for the wedding. I learned later that Paul had wanted to get out of it, but his father had forced him to keep his word. This marriage was a great mistake, but *Mektoub!* . . . It took place on 22 September and Paul and his wife took the train back to Tunis the same day.

My husband and I, my children and mother-in-law all got back at the beginning of October. The house was full to bursting; we had to have a ceiling put in the little laundry and use it as a bedroom. Louis slept in the dining-room and Marie-Louise-Taos in her grandmother's room, under the telephone. Paul and Charlotte had their bed in a sort of alcove that we used as a store-room. I kept my bedroom, where Noël and René slept.

When Jean came home on holiday from the training college, he slept in the kitchen, where we made him up a bed. But we hoped that Paul's business would do well, and that he'd go and live somewhere else.

We celebrated Christmas 1922. Paul bought a turkey which we

---

* Paul had had an unhappy love-affair, after which he let his grandmother persuade him – on the rebound – that he ought to marry a girl from our own locality. This whole drama is developed and transposed in Marie-Louise-Taos' novel, *Rue des Tambourins*.

roasted. Winter went by. Then Easter. The atmosphere in the house was more than flesh and blood could bear. My mother-in-law told all and sundry that I ill-treated my daugter-in-law, Charlotte. Lla Djohra brought her back fruit from the market, and Paul also brought oranges and dates which he kept in his room. I stuck this out for a long time, but finally I exploded: 'When you bring in something that you've no intention of giving to the little ones, at least don't let them see it!' Then, one fine day, Paul announced that he'd found premises in the rue Flatters. He moved all his grocery business out and kept the room to sleep in.

Louis now had his primary-school certificate. René was crawling all over the house, my daughter-in-law was expecting a baby in August. I was busy sewing in Lla Djohra's room when I heard Paul come in and go out again and I caught the sound of sobbing. I hurried to my daughter-in-law's room: Charlotte had collapsed, weeping bitterly. I questioned her: I learned that Paul was sailing for France that same evening.

I immediately telephoned my husband. He went to the port and caught Paul just as he was embarking. He brought him back home. There was a terrible scene. All the money we had put into the business was lost. Paul had two thousand francs on him which his father took away. He was not able to leave for Paris till the following Saturday, after he'd brought back all the shelves from the grocery shop. It was the month of May.

That same year, at more or less this time, my brother-in-law Abbas sent his son Maklouf to board with the White Fathers in Kherrata, where his young uncles were already. In addition, he and Belkacem decided to bring their father to Tunis, as he was going to divorce Zahra. My father-in-law would live for six months with us and six months with his other son, Abbas. So the two brothers sent Ahmed-ou-Amrouche a railway pass, and he joined us in Tunis.

Charlotte gave birth to her son Marcel on 6 or 7 August 1923. The birth was quite normal, in spite of the doctor's pessimism.

Life was intolerable for me in this house, which was no longer my home. Henri was doing his military service. Jean was still at the training college. Marie-Louise-Taos was ill: all her limbs were stiff and I had to rub her joints three or four times a day with camphorated oil; my mother-in-law declared that the smell upset her, so I took the child's bed into my room.

That year was the most catastrophic of any that I spent in the rue de la Rivière house. Fortuitously, one of Belkacem's friends, a man named Brizini, was to leave for Kabylia, so I persuaded Charlotte to take this opportunity of going back to her father in Ighil-Ali, where she'd be much more comfortable than with us; so she left. Then I persuaded my father-in-law to go back to his wife Zahra, the mother of his young children and his favourite. I worked on him for weeks on end to get him to agree. Finally, he gave way, on condition that we wouldn't leave him in the lurch. I promised everything he wanted, provided that he would leave. My mother-in-law accused me of turning him out, just as I'd turned my daughter-in-law out, but I didn't weaken. At last we had some room at home.

From the day that Charlotte left, my mother-in-law obstinately refused to do anything in the house. 'You've got rid of the person who should be doing the work,' she said, 'now you do it by yourself, I'll look after your baby!' So I hadn't come to the end of my troubles.

Influenced by his mother and his brother Abbas, my husband determined to bring Paul and Charlotte back. Consequently, he spent every evening after leaving the office in a flour mill, studying the machinery, so that he could set one up for Paul, either in Tunis or in Ighil-Ali. However many times I told him his son would let him down, I made no impression on him. All Paul's creditors pounced on us: the cheese merchant, the potato merchant, even a trader who had sold him a piece of furniture came to repossess it. We had to settle with all these people, sign agreements and pay them off.

In March 1924, my husband announced that his scheme was now finished. Paul would become a miller in Ighil-Ali; he would leave with Lla Djohra and Paul would return from Paris and join them there, as Belkacem had sent him the money for the fare. My husband took Charlotte's trunk and the clothes that she'd left with us. It was 20 April 1924. 'You're leaving,' I told my mother-in-law, 'but wash your feet on the threshold, as it's the last time you'll see Tunis!'

I remained alone with my children, with Henri still with his regiment, Jean at the training college; that left Louis and Noël at school, and René in his cradle. As for Marie-Louise-Taos, we sent her to the open-air school in Ariana for a few days, but she couldn't get used to it.

So Paul returned to Kabylia, saw his wife and the child he'd never seen, and his grandmother, then came back to Tunis. He hadn't spent all the money sent for his fare and he gave me what he had left, saying, 'You keep it, you never know.' There were stormy scenes between my husband and myself; I told Paul categorically that we weren't prepared to part with our modest little house back home, that we'd had so much trouble to build and pay for, just to take over a chancy business with millstones and machinery that we wouldn't know what to do with, as I was sure Paul wouldn't remain in Ighil-Ali, nor in Tunis, now that he'd seen Paris!

In the end Paul realised I was right. To raise a little money I made him sell all the useless old articles that I could find about the house: his bike, wooden planks, the shelving from his grocery store. By adding my savings we managed to raise three hundred francs. I let him take one of Henri's suits. One Saturday towards the end of May, Paul booked his berth on the boat. I had rolled out five kilos of *couscous* for him to give to a friend. Jean came from the training college to say goodbye. Paul was never to see North Africa again, but he thanked me for having urged him to leave! At last I was alone with my children, but my husband's defeat rankled with him for a long time.

Jean fell ill a short time before he was due to sit his exams. I went to bring him home from the college: he had a persistent fever, probably due to sunstroke. The doctor let him sit his exams, although he still ran a temperature and had to be stuffed with aspirins. He came second.* He took a job in the railway workshops during the holidays, to earn enough money to buy a new suit.

In October, Louis started at the technical college and Jean was appointed to the primary school in Sousse. Henri, who'd finished his

* His sister, Marguerite Taos Amrouche (Marie-Louise-Taos), adds a note to her mother's story, saying that her memory is that Jean came top of the list, but 'a native' couldn't be allowed to come first (D.S.B.).

military service, wanted to join Paul in Paris. He was provided with six shirts, a few pairs of underpants, a suit, a sports outfit and two pairs of shoes; he was given the money for the fare and he left. That was the second departure.

Marie-Louise and Noël were still sickly and the rue de la Rivière neighbourhood didn't really suit us. One day my husband's eye was caught by an advertisement in the *Tunis Despatch*. There was a little house for sale in Carthage. We went to see it on 1 January 1925, but we realised that to get to school the children would have to travel by the electric train, for which we had no concessions. So we fell back on the southern suburbs.

Most of the railway employees had built villas cheaply, but we wanted a house that was ready built, so that we could move in as soon as possible.

We found something suitable in the avenue Stephen-Pichon, in Maxula-Radès, opposite the Girls' Hostel, a four-roomed house with a good-sized garden, but we would have to brick up two windows as the house next door had been sold and the new owner insisted that the windows overlooking his property should be blocked up. We agreed to this. But God had something better in store for us! As it happened, the vendor changed his mind, but he let us know about the house that we are living in to this day.

We went to look at it on 25 May 1925. René, who was only three, made a terrible scene; he wouldn't get off the train and began to scream when I lifted him down by force.

I shall never forget my first impressions of that garden. There were flowers, flowers everywhere, flowers such as I'd never seen since my childhood in the Taddert-ou-Fella garden. I was in seventh heaven, even before I examined the house which looked rather small; there were three large rooms and one very tiny one, as a part of it had been taken up to make a passage; a kitchen, veranda and a lumber-room. The laundry was in an outhouse, as was the lavatory. There was a loft above the kitchen. It was big enough for us, as we were no longer such a large family.

I told my husband to conclude the purchase. Perhaps if we'd been more businesslike, or not in such a hurry, we might have got it for less. But we didn't know that the owner was forced to sell at any price as he'd built another house.

It was agreed that we would buy the house for twenty-nine thousand francs, putting down a deposit of ten thousand and paying the remaining nineteen thousand in yearly instalments over five years.

We hoped to sell the house in the rue de la Rivière to pay for the one in Radès, but we couldn't find a buyer to suit us, and we had to let it to my brother-in-law Abbas, who'd left the rue El Korchani.

I was never sorry we left the rue de la Rivière. I'd never been happy there, and the misery I'd experienced greatly exceeded the joys. Nevertheless, I'd lived there for seven years, seen three of my sons grow up and become men, and I can still see Paul and Henri dancing in the large dining-room.

We packed all our belongings on the night of 24 June, as the *arabas* were coming early the next morning. We'd dismantled the beds and slept on the mattresses put down in the dining-room. We were asleep when Jean rang the doorbell. He had come from Sousse to take his fourth-year exam. His friend Marcel Reggui was with him.*

I was up at dawn and had already cooked the chicken on the gas stove, so that we'd have something to eat at midday: the *arabas* had been loaded with our furniture. A few things remained that we hoped to fetch later, in particular two little cupboards that had been fixed to the wall in my bedroom. We never got them back as they were seized by the bailiffs when they took possession of my brother-in-law's furniture.

When the *arabas* had left, we caught the eleven o'clock train and reached our new home at midday. The previous owners had already moved out.

Jean stayed to dine with us that day. How proud he was when he came in from the garden with a plate of strawberries and sour figs, saying, 'So useful to have one's own garden!'

* This was Jean Amrouche's oldest friend, an Algerian born in Guelma, converted to Christianity, whose family originally came from Gabès in Tunisia. He became a high school teacher, and at the time this book was published, was Chairman of the People's Association for Art and Culture in Orleans, where he went to live when he retired.

Radès: A Haven at Last

I shall not say very much about my life in Radès, as it is familiar to all my children. I shall simply recall some memories.

The first years were very hard, I took the household finances in hand, as I did every time we had to tighten our belts. From 1925 to 1930 we had very heavy debts to repay. To raise the first ten thousand francs, we had to go to the moneylender, Burgel, taking out a mortgage on the rue de la Rivière house at a very high interest; Henri and Paul gave us some help. Every fortnight Paul cabled us fifty francs out of his pay, and when Henri was at the North African Agency, he sent us a hundred and fifty francs a month. In addition, I kept the food as simple as possible: thick soups with noodles and dried vegetables – broad beans, split peas or small white beans; there were generous helpings, however, and as much fresh white bread as anyone could eat.

Jean spent the month of July with us, sleeping in the little room. On 1 August he told me, 'Mother, I'm leaving for Paris, too. From now till 1 October, I'll see what I can find to do.' He was only nineteen. He was the third of my sons to be taken from me by that terrible, wonderful city.

I cannot recall much of all those years: the children went to school; René, who was still very young, remained at home; he would perch on the main gatepost and watch the passers-by. He was golden-brown, like a nectarine, with a forest of curly hair, his head covered in ringlets, and sometimes when he caught sight of a lady, he would say, 'Will you give me a sweetie, lady?'

He jumped down from his perch as soon as Noël came home from school. Then he climbed the almond trees, filled his pockets with nuts and said, 'One pocket for you, one for me.' Of all the children, he and Jean stayed at home with me the longest. When he was a bit bigger, René would look at the clock and say, 'Nel will be coming out of school, I'm going to meet him.' And off he'd go to meet Noël.

We had no more problems with our health: we had fresh air, fruit, vegetables and as much bread as we wanted. I bought clothes for the children at the *Gagne-Petit* (Children's Economy Shop): strong warm velveteen coats for winter, and shoes. Marie-Louise had a velours coat. We were not free from financial problems, but I could feel at home, at last; for the first time since my marriage I didn't have to put up with anyone's disapproval: Kabyles, arriving from back home, didn't descend on us anymore.

In October we heard from Jean that he'd passed the entrance examination for Versailles, where he would prepare for the Ecole Normale in Saint-Cloud. I heaved a sigh of relief. For the next twelve months we need not worry about him, afterwards, God would provide.

I can still see them all sitting at the round table in the dining-room, on a Sunday, when we had a *couscous*: Louis, Marie-Louise-Taos, Noël, René and Jean home for the holidays. Jean inciting Noël, who was a terrible tease, to bait Louis. Noël starts on him: 'Louis, you run like a hippopotamus!' To which Louis retorts, 'Look out, Ahès!' (Noël was inclined to hunch his shoulders, so we called him Hessouna, or Ahès for short, after a hunchback who lived near us in the rue de la Rivière.)

The children would also sit on the floor in René's room, which he shared with Louis and Noël, and play dominoes, but Noël used to cheat by blocking out the black dots with bread. I would occasionally hear quarrels and then I went and distributed clouts all round.

Louis adored playing *belote* (a card game rather like bezique), and he used to play for hours on end. But we discovered rather late in the day that he often missed school and intercepted the notes sent complaining about his absence. I did not see my son Louis grow up: for me he was always the pampered baby that had to be carried on my back till he was three. It was years before he learned to speak properly, especially in Kabyle; when he was already a youngster he still mispronounced his words, like a baby, which made his brothers tease him. Lla Djohra had spoilt him badly, more than Marie-Louise-Taos and Noël, but she'd also taught him certain bad habits, like listening at doors.

I hadn't been back to Kabylia since 1922. In 1927 I had a bad attack of flu and as usual I didn't look after myself, so one day I couldn't get out of bed. My husband had to get a maid and it was decided that I should go to spend the holidays in Kabylia.

On my arrival I found many empty places: cousin Chérif-ou-Amrouche was dead, as were other cousins of my father-in-law. I was extremely fond of Chérif, a gentle, dignified man, and for a long time I could recall the sight of his tall figure. I never saw Chérif angry in all the seven or eight years I spent in Ighil-Ali. He was always ready to stand up for us, when any of the others ran us down; Bachi-ou-Youssef,* the husband of Lla Djohra's sister Aldja, was dead, as well as Madani's two daughters and her son Mohamed. Old uncle Hemma was living with his sister – my mother-in-law – in our house, where he stayed till his death.

A few days after my arrival, Henri and Jean came from France to join us, but Henri didn't stay long. He was getting married in December of that year.

When the holidays were over, we returned to Radès. Jeanne,† my maid, had looked after the house. Jean returned to Saint-Cloud.

In November, Louis told us he was going to work for the Tunis Municipality. We had to make the best of a bad job. We'd have preferred him to continue his studies and go in for teaching. He was still as innocent of the world as a child, but he got into bad company from whom he learned quickly.

I can't remember whether it was in 1927 or '28 that Marie-Louise passed her school certificate. In September 1927, my husband managed to sell the house in the rue de la Rivière to his friend Brizini, who paid him ten thousand francs down and the rest over ten years. So we were able to settle all our debts. In October 1928 Jean returned to Tunis to do his military service, as he'd qualified as a high school teacher at Saint-Cloud.

As my husband was eligible for free travel, he went that summer to Lourdes and then on to Paris, where he took Paul's wife and son back to him. Marie-Louise-Taos went with him.

---

* Jean Amrouche wrote a short story of which this Bachi is the hero.
† She was an Italian, married to an Arab; she'd converted to Islam, taken the name Habiba, and always wore a veil out of doors. In Marguerite Taos's novel, *Rue des Tambourins*, she appears as Alba.

That same year, 1928, Louis left his job with the Municipality and decided to leave for Paris. We wrote to Paul, asking for his advice, and he telegraphed back, 'Send parcel', so we despatched Louis. It was a great wrench for me, as I'd foreseen everything except separation from Louis, whom I considered somewhat retarded: I wanted to keep him with me, so that I could watch over him.

Jean was doing his military service in Bizerta but he came back to Tunis in January to attend the course for cadets. He stayed for six months, during which we saw a lot of him at home; Marie-Louise's school-friends often waited for him to help them solve their algebra problems.

He entered Saint-Maixent Military College, where he stayed till 1929. He left there as a handsome second lieutenant and people who met him used to ask my husband, 'Is that handsome second lieutenant your son?' and my husband was very proud of him. In January 1930 he was appointed to the Sousse High School.

Paul's family had increased by a little daughter, Monique. We thought that peace had been restored to this household, now comfortably installed in the boulevard de Sebastopol, when we received alarming news concerning the baby's health and Paul's carryings-on. Such was the state of affairs after he'd been back together with his wife for two years. My husband took advantage of his new travel pass and went to Paris in May. Jean and Marie-Louise-Taos joined him for the holidays. They all confirmed that little Monique was seriously ill. I suggested to Belkacem that he should send Paul's wife and children back to us, for Monique to get well again. Charlotte arrived at the beginning of October 1930. The child would certainly have died if she had stayed in Paris.

But there was not enough room in the Radès house and when Jean came home on All Saints' Day, for the half-term holidays, he had to sleep in his father's bed, while I slept head-to-tail with Marie-Louise-Taos. René took his bed into his father's room and Noël made do with the hard sofa in the dining-room.

The following day Jean said that this situation couldn't continue. Charlotte wrote to her parents asking if she could go back to them in Ighil-Ali. She returned to them some time in December.

Then we decided to enlarge the house. When Jean spent his holidays at home Marie-Louise-Taos had to let him have her little room opposite mine – that small room rich in memories, where she did her homework and worked on her problems: occasionally I'd helped her. She'd already passed her school certificate.

We got tenders from three Italian contractors. Finally we decided to buy the materials ourselves and to engage a builder who we paid by the day. We demolished the outhouses which were up against the kitchen, keeping one wall which turned out to be damp and insanitary. In a relatively short time, three rooms and a glazed-in veranda had been built. We also had an outside staircase, leading to the roof. We had begun work at Christmas and by Easter everything was completed.

In September 1931 Jean announced his engagement and brought the girl to be introduced to us, with her mother.

Marie-Louise, Noël and René had spent the holidays in Ighil-Ali, without me. One week after they returned, René went down with a very high temperature. The doctor diagnosed typhoid fever. On 1 October Noël went to school in the morning, but that same evening he had to be put to bed. Charlotte and her two young ones had come back from Kabylia with my children. My daughter-in-law took over the household, while I looked after the invalids. The ice-packs on their heads had to be changed every few hours, right through the day and night. Marie-Louise did the shopping, but then she fell ill in turn. She was treated for malaria, but in fact she'd contracted typhoid too. I struggled for three months. On 1 November we called in three doctors in consultation. They said I should stop the baths but keep on applying cooling packs.

René was the worst affected: an artificially provoked fixation abscess saved him. Noël recovered fairly quickly from the physical effects of the illness, but I got the impression that morally he was never the same again.

Louis had to return to Tunis to do his military service. Before he went back to barracks he also helped fetch ice.

During all this wretched, anxious period, my little blonde granddaughter, Monique, was a ray of sunshine. She was not quite three, but strong and sturdy on her little legs. She also wanted to help; she would bring me, pressed against her little stomach, the ice-pack to put on the head of one or other of the children, and she'd take Marie-Louise her herb-tea, saying, 'Nice, auntie, drink!'

Her mother was a model of devotion, and I don't know how I'd have managed without her at my side. Nobody would have helped us, as everyone was afraid of catching the disease. From the end of September to the end of December, I never got out of my clothes or lay down for a night's sleep. When René was out of danger, I had to sit up with Marie-Louise-Taos, who had just fallen ill. In January 1932 they could all get up at last.

During the whole time this illness lasted Jean came from Sousse every Wednesday evening and stayed till dawn on Friday morning. He was always at our side when we were in trouble. The new wing of the house was very useful as now each of my children, as well as my daughter-in-law with her children, could have a room. Her little Marcel went off early every morning to fetch the milk and then the bread, before setting off for school. Jean got married in May, but only Marie-Louise attended the wedding ceremony. The young couple came to supper with us and had a short honeymoon in Hammamet.

On 24 June 1932 Charlotte went back to Ighil-Ali, to join her sister who was visiting from her home in Morocco. That year we were all entitled to free travel to France. My daughter said, 'Why don't you come with us, Mother?' My husband had made a vow to take René and Noël to Lourdes. Mme Benquet, my neighbour, who was a dressmaker, cut out three dresses for me, I made myself some underclothes and set off with my children and Belkacem. Henri had invited us to stay with him in Paris in the boulevard des Batignolles. We caught the boat at the end of July. Marie-Louise-Taos and I went on to Paris, my husband and the two boys to Lourdes. I hadn't seen Paul for eight years, and it was seven years since I'd seen Henri. We were made very welcome, but I knew Henri and his wife were not well-off and I insisted on paying for our share of the food. The flat was roomy, but they had to share the tap on the landing and the lavatory with the other tenants on the first floor. My daughter-in-law Marcelle's bedroom and the dining-room were big and airy. Marie-Louise slept in Henri's study.

After their pilgrimage to Lourdes, my husband and the children came on to Paris and slept in Paul's big flat, which was still sparsely furnished. We spent three weeks in Paris. We went on some excursions: to Lisieux, Chartres Cathedral, the Palace of Versailles. I tried to persuade Paul to take his wife and children back but he refused categorically, saying he'd decided to send what money he could afford, but under no circumstances would he resume married life with Charlotte. I explained that I'd found that year particularly difficult and that my youngest children didn't always get on with his, and that I had to put my own first.

We left for Tunis after Assumption Day (15 August), travelling via Algiers and Ighil-Ali. We stopped at Maison-Carrée to visit Father Justrob, and found Fathers Duchène, Dehuisserre and Vidal there too: that was the last time we met. After three days in Ighil-Ali we were very happy to be met at Radès station by Ali, our gardener, who'd looked after the house while we were away. He took our luggage in his wheelbarrow and we were back home.

Louis finished his military service. I persuaded him to spend a few days at home to let him rest, I fitted him out with some shirts, underpants and socks. I gave him a suit that was still in very good condition which Jean had passed on to his father, and he left with other soldiers, to be demobilised in Paris, so that he wouldn't have to pay his own fare. He never returned to North Africa!

Noël, René and Marie-Louise-Taos were the only ones left now. Noël had passed his primary-school certificate and decided to attend the Radès Secondary School to get his school-leaving certificate. I wasn't keen on sending him to the Aláoui Collège in Tunis, as the experience with Louis had been enough for me. René was still a child, he was ten.

I didn't see Noël growing up, any more than I had Louis. He was fifteen, but he was precocious. He went about with a lot of youngsters of his own age, or even older. In May 1933, he started playing truant. He set off in the morning with his satchel, but spent his time roaming about the streets. If he met anyone who expressed surprise at seeing him, he said, 'I got hurt by a football.' It was no use my imploring him, pointing out how much harm he was doing himself by not continuing his studies, I was wasting my breath. He declared, 'I want to go to

Paris!' 'To do what?' 'I'll work with Paul.' The latter had just taken out a lease on a restaurant in Montmartre, *le Moustique*, of which he had high hopes. Noël's father wrote to Paul who replied, 'Send him.' Noël embarked at the beginning of July. He spent three months in Paris and returned with Jean at the end of September. In October, Noël, Marie-Louise and René went back to school. But in November Marie-Louise fell ill and Noël took advantage of this to leave school for good. He wanted to start work, his father had to find him a job, but what was most important, he had to have money. Wherever I hid the money for the housekeeping, he managed to find it and helped himself. My husband decided to send him to Paris where, he thought, his brothers would fix him up with something.

Henri suggested that he would get him apprenticed to a hairdresser if we could send him an allowance. So Noël went to stay with him. But Henri didn't keep him long, as he was impossible to put up with, in spite of the three or four hundred francs a month we sent him. He went to the *Moustique*, where cousin Bélaïd and Louis had a room. Paul persuaded Henri to give him a mattress. I had given him a suitcase full of clothes and an overcoat in good condition that Paul had left with me.

In July 1934 we set off again for Paris, where we'd asked the children to find us a furnished flat for a month. We left an Arab to look after the house and garden in Radès, paying him a salary of one hundred francs. Louis was doing another period of army service at the camp in Sissone, Noël had found a job, Paul and Henri were both working at the printing-press.

In October Marie-Louise-Taos passed her senior certificate and we asked the Company for a loan so that we could send her to France to continue her studies. We even found her a room in a women's hostel in Paris. But she couldn't settle down to the life there and came back to Radès after two months.*

* Marie-Louise's experiences in the women's hostel formed the inspiration for her novel, *Jacinthe noire* (Black Hyacinth) which she published in 1947 under the name of Taos Amrouche. She tells of the disturbing effect the arrival of a Tunisian girl has on the claustrophobic atmosphere of the Catholic hostel and some of its residents. This was the first work published in French by a North African woman (D.S.B.).

In May 1935 my husband had to retire: this caused me a great problem; he was only fifty-three and was not interested in the garden. I sent him to spend a month in Kabylia. On his return he went to spend a few weeks in Paris.

I thought that if we bought a second-hand car, it would give him an interest and stop him getting bored, so for five thousand francs we acquired a nice Citroën 7CV, the '7-9' as it was then called.* Belkacem took driving lessons and obtained his licence.

In October 1935 Marie-Louise was appointed junior teacher at the Radès boarding-school. From December 1935 to May 1936, we had some very happy times. Jean came for the Christmas holidays with his colleague and friend, Marcel Brémond, who drove us to Carthage, Sidi-Bou-Saïd and Hammamet. I hadn't been out of the house for such a long time, so for me it was a real joy to step out of my front door, get in the car and go off on a voyage of discovery. On Thursdays and Sundays, when Marie-Louise had her free days, we picked her up at the school and went off with her and René, without any fixed destination. We took a picnic lunch with us – a big omelette or some cooked brains – to eat out in the country, on the way to Bizerta, or in Djebel-Rssas, Hammamet, Korbous, or Hammam-Plage-les-Pins.

But it was too good to last. One day we crashed the car. There was a loud bump and I heard my husband say, 'That's done it! We've overturned!' It was 19 May. We'd been to Medjez-el-Bab; as Belkacem tried to avoid a car coming towards us, our car had slewed round and skidded into a ditch. Fortunately, René, who wasn't hurt, managed to scramble out through the windscreen and call some passers-by to help us. I had a cut above my forehead which was bleeding profusely; I was taken to the village clinic, where a doctor stitched up the wound. My husband had been hit in the chest by the steering-wheel but seemed to be all right; however, by the time we got him home his teeth were chattering as he'd caught a chill.

---

* The car was christened 'Peg-out!', Marie-Louise tells us, adding, 'My father who, all his life, had put his children first, finally rebelled. One day, in the garden, when my mother pointed out that all the children weren't yet off their hands, he exploded, raising his hands to heaven and shouting "You can peg out, all of you, but I'll have my car!" And that was the end of the matter.'

The next day René went for the doctor who said that Belkacem's condition was more serious than mine: he had congestion of the lungs. We telegraphed to Jean who came the same evening. We let Marie-Louise know – fortunately she'd not been with us at the time of the accident. She hurried back to Radès, with her friend Nanou Carlini. My condition got worse: I developed erisipelis. For days on end I suffered from pustules in my ears. In a fortnight we were both out of danger. The car had been towed away by Caccio, the garage-owner. It was repaired and sold. From then on, my husband who had smoked all his life, from the age of fifteen, gave up altogether. It's an ill wind that blows no good.

On 23 June we took the boat for France and went to stay in La Varenne-Saint-Hilaire, where Paul had rented a house with its own grounds, which was large enough for all of us to stay. He entertained us royally. The following year we returned for the 1937 Exposition, and I shall never forget this house and garden, where there were so many roses of every colour and species, where there was so much happiness, prosperity, abundance. Louis was living with Paul and he, too, benefited from this lovely environment. I can still see the fine red Hamilcar that Paul drove. He took us to the Exposition, to Andelys, Rouen, Gros-Bois, and the Berthier Princes' Castle. He went to endless lengths to please us, even though a business deal he'd been counting on had turned out badly. We left at the end of August, as I was anxious about the house in Radès, which I'd left with people I didn't wholly trust.

Paul drove us to the Gare de Lyons, but he didn't come into the station as he had to stay with his car. As I was kissing him goodbye he said, 'You'll be back in two or three years and you'll find great changes!' I never saw him again. Jeanne, his companion, and Louis had reserved seats for us. When Louis kissed me I noticed that he pressed his lips very hard against my cheek. I never saw him again.

Marie-Louise stayed behind in Paris.

In October 1937 Paul was transferred to Tunis. Then things started moving fast. Noël, who had foolishly enlisted in the army for five years, after getting himself into serious trouble, contracted tuberculosis, that scourge which had ravaged the Amrouche family in Ighil-Ali.

Louis also caught it and was the first to die, on 20 August 1939, in the Brévannes Sanatorium.

Paul telegraphed us the terrible news. Jean flew over to attend the funeral. Paul, in obedience to my husband's wishes, was preparing to bring the body back to Ighil-Ali when war broke out. That was only the beginning of our misfortunes. To the defeat of France, the bombing, the Occupation, the misery, the starvation, were added two new personal losses: Paul died during the Exodus from Paris on 16 June 1940, and Noël died at the hospital, on 10 July 1940. We received news of this double blow from a card sent from the Occupied to the Unoccupied Zone.*

However, the burden of this pre-war period was lightened by a project in which Marie-Louise-Taos, Jean and I had been involved for some months: this was to translate into French the Berber songs which had been passed down to us from our ancestors, and which had helped me to support my exile and lull my sorrows. It was such a joy to me to see my children finally show enthusiasm for this cultural heritage. Among Jean's friends, who also taught at the Carnot High School in Tunis, and who came to eat *couscous* with us and pick our oranges, Armand Guibert was the one who was the most closely associated with our research; he published in his collection *Monomotapa* the volume of poems that Jean translated, *Chants Berbères de Kabylie* (Berber Songs from Kabylia), which won the Carthage Prize.

Meanwhile, Marie-Louise had found a vocation singing the Berber songs I had taught her. The war did not prevent her continuing her career and, after appearing at the Fez Congress, she was invited to the Casa Velasquez in Spain, in May 1941. There, in Madrid, she met her husband the artist André Bourdil. Just before the Americans landed, she left Spain for Radès, pregnant with her daughter Laurence and accompanied by André. Henri, too, managed to escape from the Occupied Zone, with his wife and twins, and took refuge with us in Radès.

Jean, who had got divorced and was now married to Suzanne, gave up his flat in Tunis which overlooked the port and so was too exposed

---

* As Noël's brothers were either dead or dispersed, and his parents could not be contacted in Tunisia, he was buried in a common grave. Laurence Bourdil informs me that Paul had in fact committed suicide (D.S.B).

to bombs, and he also came to live with us.

During the grievous hours of the Occupation, at the time of great danger, the good Lord in his mercy had grouped all my living children around me. If we had had to die, we would all have died together.

Since then, peace has returned. Germany has been beaten and driven out. The family is dispersed once more, each one to his or her own fortunes.

My brown locks have turned white. The big house is empty, its occupants have all left, except for my life's companion, with whom I have celebrated forty-seven years of marriage.

I returned to Ighil-Ali after an absence of eight years: there were many, many graves, as many among our own relatives from the upper village as among the Christian families (Merzoug, Chlili, Sliman, Saïd Guâmara, his mother and sister), three houses shut up, four counting our own.

Of the Amrouche family home, which I saw from a distance, only empty ruins remained; the shutters of the upper storey, where I thought forty years ago that I would spend the rest of my life, hung down wretchedly, and of all that Amrouche family, old grandfather Ahmed was the only one left. And I said to myself, 'Vanity of Vanities, all is Vanity, save God and the little good we have been able to do!'

When I got back to this house in Radès, where I have been living now for twenty-two years, I only had one wish, and that was to return to that abandoned house in Ighil-Ali. Will this wish be granted to me? That is a secret known only to God. I now close this notebook, to which I have committed the brief story of my life.

I have written it all in one month. It is 28 August, I have worked quickly, you never know . . .

I am old, worn out, but I have still the heart and soul of a child, ready to redress wrongs and defend the oppressed.

I never saw my school again, I don't know what became of it, but in my memory the enchanted image of my youth is still vivid. I can still see the flower-strewn path, the wild roses, the honeysuckle, the festoons of clematis, the foaming waters of the cascade, the flower-covered banks of my stream and the carpets of buttercups.

When, on summer nights, I hear the frogs croaking, I see before me the garden in La Varenne-Saint-Hilaire with its climbing roses. I can say with the poet, 'On that day, at that spot, for one day, I was happy.'

I nearly forgot my garden in Toujal, with its vine-covered arbour, and Fort-National on the horizon, with its red tiles and white ramparts!

I have just re-read this long account and I see that I have omitted to say that I always remained 'the Kabyle woman'; never, in spite of the forty years I have spent in Tunisia, in spite of my basically French education, never have I been able to become a close friend of any French people, nor of Arabs. I remain for ever the eternal exile, the woman who has never felt at home anywhere.

Now, more than ever, I yearn to be in my own homeland, in my own village, among those of my own race, with the same language, the same mentality, the same superstitious, simple souls, athirst for freedom and independence, and with the spirit of Jugurtha!*

I dedicate these pages to my son Jean: I have written this story for him, so that he may know what my mother and I suffered and laboured, in order that, one day, the Berber poet Jean Amrouche could be born.

1–31 August 1946
Maxula-Radès

* Jugurtha, King of Numidia (*c*. 154-104 BC) is a symbol of African independence. Sallust tells the story of his heroic resistance to the Romans, by whom however he was defeated and brought in triumph to Rome, where he died in prison (D.S.B.).

IV

Epilogue

This is the epilogue to the story of my life that I wrote in Maxula-Radès, in August 1946, to commemorate the fiftieth anniversary of my leaving school in Taddert-ou-Fella, in Kabylia. I dedicated that account to my son Jean, to whom I entrusted it. I tried to re-open it in Ighil-Ali in 1953, but I realised that Papa disliked the idea and as I didn't want to make him unhappy, I put the notebook back in the drawer of which he alone had the key, hung on his watch-chain.

I dedicate this sequel to my daughter, Taos, Marie-Louise Amrouche, in memory of our forefathers, of the old abandoned family home, in memory of the land of Kabylia which we shall probably never see again.

In memory of her dead father and brothers, I dedicate to her everything that I have been able to recall, these clumsy lines, for my sight gets weaker and my hands tremble, and it costs me such an effort to write legibly. I have known so many misfortunes.

When I started writing this long story, I was in Tunisia, in the house in Radès, six miles from Tunis. But by dint of economies and deprivations, we'd managed to build our house in the Christian settlement, near the Amrouche family home in Ighil-Ali.

The children, my mother-in-law and I used to spend our holidays there; this is the region that Taos described under the name of 'Thala-el-Hadj', the mountain garden of grandfather Ahmed, in that section of her novel, *Rue des Tambourins*, that she entitles 'La Source des pélerins' (The Pilgrims' Spring).

My husband had always wanted to end his days in his native village. When he took retirement in 1935, our youngest son René was still at school and so we had to stay in Tunis to let him finish his education. All the older ones had already left home to settle in Paris.

After the 1939-40 war* the house was empty once more and we could think of returning to Kabylia. All the children had gone, some were dead, the others were in France. In 1953, by a miracle, we finally found a buyer for our house in Radès. This was a man who owned a house in Hammamet.

René had just been appointed as a reporter to Radio Tunis. On 15 May 1953 we were finally ready to leave Tunisia. The Tunisian Railway Company did things in style: they put a railway truck at our disposal, free of charge, to transport all our goods. We arrived in Ighil-Ali. During our last, long absence, many of our relatives had died. Lla Djohra and her brother Hemma had gone, but grandfather Ahmed was still alive, although his legs were paralysed. His wife Zahra looked after him; she did her best to keep him clean, although she was in poor health herself. He lacked for nothing. She said to me, 'His name is great. Visitors must not find the sight of him unpleasant.' He was greatly respected and people came to greet him because of his age and infirmity.

Charlotte's father, El Mouhouv-ou-Ouari, was still of this world, but greatly weakened. We moved into our house, using the two rooms on the upper storey for our living-quarters; leaving the ground floor for a workshop. Belkacem installed his carpenter's bench with all his hammers and tools.

We put all the old furniture which we'd brought from Tunisia into the big rooms upstairs. My husband called in the builder to repair the roof and the ceilings. The balcony was enlarged and roofed over, with two large pillars to support the construction. Belkacem had two bay-windows put into the wall facing the street, to give us more light, and he bought a stove to heat the house. The balcony became a glazed veranda about forty feet long by ten feet wide, out of which he took ten feet for the kitchen, which had a window on the side nearest the post office. He had a lavatory put in near to the stairs and installed running water and electricity. The fig tree which grandfather had grafted still grew in the courtyard, with the olive tree overhanging the stone staircase. Belkacem had the enclosing wall repaired and all the other walls rough rendered, and the whole place was made very habitable. We did our own

* *Sic.* The author is referring to the Second World War (D.S.B.).

cooking at home, as Papa didn't like curious eyes on him. We could get all our requirements in the village: the baker delivered bread to the house. We spent the rest of that year very quietly. In the evenings we used to go for a walk along the road, towards the station.

But it was too good to last. In 1954 the Algerian War broke out.

In January 1954 my father-in-law Ahmed-ou-Amrouche died. It had been snowing all night. We sent telegrams to his children who were living in Tunis. The postal van, which was to bring them back from the station, couldn't even get there as the snow was too deep.

My husband had slept at the upper village to be near his father, who died during the night, just as he was lifting a spoonful of *couscous* to his lips. His two other sons walked through the snow from the station, and arrived exhausted and soaked through. Grandfather could not be buried till the next day; he had always been anxious to be accorded a funeral worthy of the name he bore: his wishes were respected.

That same week El Mouhouv-ou-Ouari died. I was in bed with a severe bronchitis and could not attend the funeral. Charlotte arrived from Algiers and came to see me; we had an argument about Henri and she left again without saying goodbye.

The years 1954 and 1955 were fairly peaceful. But trouble had been brewing ever since the Arris affair and the murder of the schoolteacher. Confusion reigned in the mines and on the farms. Gradually, army units were stationed in the villages and the *maquis* was formed. There was a curfew at seven in the evening and killings on both sides.

In February 1956 the White Fathers declared that all the Christian families should be evacuated, as they ran the risk of being massacred by the Muslims. In the general panic, we had to leave our homes and go anywhere we could.

As every winter, I was ill in bed. I had to get up, pack, take all our stocks of food over to the nuns, and the next morning I got into Hubert's lorry, with Sister Suzanne. The Zahouals, who were going to Tizi-Ouzou, and the Ouari couple, who were going to their daughters', had already taken their places. We spent the night with a relative, who gave us his bed. Hubert's mother, Marie-Rose, and the post-office clerk were the only Christians left in Ighil-Ali. At ten o'clock the next morning we caught the plane at Maison-Blanche. At one o'clock in the afternoon we were in Paris. It was the beginning of February 1956.

Since the children had all gone their different ways, we had been back to France on several occasions: in 1949, for our fiftieth wedding anniversary, just after Jean had gone to live in the boulevard Malesherbes. We had travelled via Manosque, where we spent a few weeks with Marie-Louise-Taos, her artist husband André Bourdil and their little daughter Laurence, who were the guests of the novelist Giono. Our golden wedding celebrations, which were held at Jean's country house in Sargé-sur-Braye (Loir et Cher), coincided with the christening of Pierre, Jean's youngest child.

Another trip had taken us to Lourdes in 1953: my husband thought that the Virgin would restore my lost faith, but Lourdes had the opposite effect: all that religiosity, all that commercialisation, was repugnant to me. What was even worse was to hear a priest talking about 'mental restriction' – in other words, lies in disguise – in referring to confession. This pilgrimage to Lourdes acquitted us of a vow taken when we sold the house in Radès.

When we landed up at Jean's in February 1956, with the temperature at minus 13°C., carrying one small suitcase, for an indefinite stay, our son could not disguise the fact that we presented him with a problem. To put us up for a holiday was one thing, to keep us for ever was quite another. As we were particularly touchy under these difficult circumstances, we were deeply hurt by Jean's suggestion that we should find separate accommodation in Paris or the suburbs.

I went to see my daugher and put her in the picture. She offered to have us, but after a few weeks we decided we'd rather go and stay in Sargé. So we left in May and spent the summer and autumn there.

We had a letter from Algeria telling us that the post-office clerk's family had returned to Ighil-Ali, so my husband, with his mind put at rest, decided to go back too. He made the necessary applications, obtained the necessary papers. In February 1957 we caught the plane for Algiers, in spite of the children's apprehensions, especially Jean's.

As I set foot on Algerian soil, I said, 'Farewell France!' My husband replied, 'You must never say to a spring, "I shall never drink again of your waters!"'

*

From March 1957 to October 1958, we experienced all the vicissitudes of war: the local population was the object of harassment by the army; the underground committed sabotage during the night and the next morning the army forced the local people to undertake the repairs. There was suffering among the civilians on both sides and my husband grew thinner by the day.

The worst day was when he was captured by the army in a round-up when he had gone out to buy bread. He was taken to the school with everyone who'd been found in the street: there had been a burst of gunfire from the cemetary, the army had given orders that everyone had to stay indoors; the soldiers picked up anyone they met. This eighty-year-old man had to stand in the sun from ten in the morning till eight at night.* I was running round the village all day, like a madwoman, not going home to eat or drink.

To the Kabyles, we were *Roumis*, renegades. They envied us the few comforts we had acquired after so much effort, privation and exile.† To the army, we were just Wogs, like all the rest.

We survived to the end of 1957; the army had taken over the lay school. The Fathers re-opened the mission schools but there was still a curfew at eight o'clock and the soldiers shot anyone they met out of doors. This was what happened to four youngsters whose dead bodies were picked up one morning. All this daily sapped my husband's strength. There was no midnight mass that Christmas. When Belkacem went to the monastery chapel, I trembled for his safety, fearing the army as much as the Kabyles.

A cyst that he had on his shoulder developed into an abscess; I had to lance it for him myself. One day I found my husband with a needle

---

* The author slightly miscalculates her husband's age. If Belkacem was eighteen when they married in 1899, he would have been seventy-six or seventy-seven (D.S.B.).

† Marguerite-Taos Amrouche adds a footnote to her mother's story. 'Members of the F.N.L. (Front de Libération Nationale) called on my father, demanding a contribution to their funds. My father opened the drawer and showed them his retirement papers. When they saw how modest his pension was, they withdrew in confusion, saying, "*Aêfuyar, a êmmi Belkacem!*" (Forgive us, Uncle Belkacem).'

and a tape measure in his hand. He said, 'I'm losing so much weight that if I don't take in my belt my trousers will fall down.'

He got around and kept himself busy, working in his workshop where he had all his tools arranged round the walls. he'd installed electricity in the kitchen. What a joy when we finally had running water in our own home: he'd had it put in on the ground floor and the upper storey. He cast concrete slabs himself to line the cesspool. When I said, 'Take things easy. You're working too hard!' he'd reply, 'I'm bored. I've got to work!'

Early in the morning, he climbed up the fig tree to pick the fruit. When I got up I found the basket of fresh figs. 'Eat!' he said. 'They're good.' And I ate them, and he was pleased.

He swept the floors and sometimes did the dusting. 'It's important,' he said, 'that people who come to see us should enter a clean house.'

He had relaid the floor-tiles himself, but he never missed a church service and the nuns relied on him for the hymns, as none of them could sing in tune. He could play the harmonium and sang the gregorian chants in a very melodious tenor voice.

There were only two of the Fathers left: Father Duplan who did the teaching, and Father Etienne for the parish duties. When Father Kérinal died from a liver complaint, Father Duplan came to ask my husband's advice. That was 3 December 1958.

So we lived, each of us as anxious and worried as the other. Then came the day when we received news of Henri's death. It was the eve of All Saints' Day (31 October). I had never heard my husband weep so hopelessly: he was inconsolable. He had a bilious attack and brought up everything he'd eaten.

He dragged on till Christmas. He hadn't been able to get his piece of meat for our Christmas meal, but the children had sent food parcels from France, sweets and delicacies, and I served him generously. He ate too much, probably: he had another upset stomach. He did not have his own teeth any more, and swallowed his food without chewing it. That day he went to church after lunch; it was cold and he hadn't digested his food. As soon as he got home he brought up everything he'd eaten – segments of orange still whole.

It was a Saturday evening, 27 December 1958. I had fallen asleep, he had come home early, but the days were short. We'd received New

Year greetings letters. There was one which upset him, and he began to cry hopelessly. When I tried to console him, he said, 'Let me cry, it gives me some relief!'

I must explain that all my life I'd worried about him, as he was subject to black-outs; suddenly, for no apparent reason, it would come over him – it happened several times at his office, once at the dentist's – and he'd tell me about it when he got home. I used to wait for him in front of our gate, whenever he was late. When he got back he'd say, 'You'll never change!' and I was so pleased to see him that I didn't answer.

Sometimes, when I woke up in the night, if I couldn't hear him breathing, I called out, '*Amrar*!'* As soon as he replied, I could go off to sleep again, with my mind at rest.

Even in the morning, when he went to mass, I was anxious until he got back. At this time, the only people living in the Christian village were the post-office clerk, with his wife and mother, Hubert and his mother, Marie-Rose, and the two Muslim families who had rented the empty houses belonging to Blanche and Marie-G'âmara. That will give you some idea of the eerie atmosphere of the place! The whole night we trembled every time we heard a noise. In spite of the locks and bolts, we were afraid of everything, and of the unknown.

The 3rd of January was a Saturday. In the evening, my husband finished reading his newspaper in front of the stove, by the light of a little paraffin lamp, as the electric pylons had been destroyed. He'd been out all day, round the village shops, at Hubert's. When the curfew sounded, he came to kiss me goodnight and went to bed, saying, 'I'll soon be asleep.'

He'd shaved carefully, so as to be ready for early mass, and he fell asleep.

Two hours later I heard him get up, saying, 'I can't breathe! I can't breathe!' I replied, 'Go out on to the balcony and get some fresh air.' I heard him repeat, 'I can't breathe!'

He went out to the stairs, to go to the lavatory; I could still hear

* *Amrar*, literally, 'master' or 'old man'; this is the way Kabyle women address their husbands, so expressing the notion of age and respect, associated with a patriarchal society like that of the Berbers.

him, and then, there was silence . . . I was worried. I got up and went in my nightdress and bare feet to see what was wrong. I found him sitting on the seat. I cried, '*Amrar! Amrar!*'

He didn't answer. I pulled on his hands and tried to lift him, but he was too heavy. I let go and ran to the kitchen window and called René Zahoual.

'René, come quick! Monsieur Amrouche is ill, I'm frightened!'

René came round to the street door which I opened to let him in. He picked up my husband in his arms and laid him down on his bed.

'Should we send for the army doctor?'

But he could feel that the heart had stopped beating. He called his mother who stayed with me. During the night I got up several times to see if he was cold and pulled the blankets over him, but he needed nothing now.

By morning I'd managed to get back to sleep for a little. The news had already spread through the village. The nuns called, when they came out from mass; they brought holy water and wound his rosary around his wrists. I was completely numb, understanding nothing that was going on. I saw the house filling up with relatives from the upper village; among them was cousin Messaoud's son, who wanted to move into our house.

Hubert had asked the army to telegraph the children in Paris, so that they could attend the funeral, but when we got no reply Father Etienne came to tell me that we must proceed with the burial without them. In fact no telegram ever reached Paris. The children didn't hear of their father's death till a fortnight later.

On Monday evening the one who had shared my life for sixty years left me for ever. For two days and two nights there had been a procession of relatives who wouldn't leave me alone, yet talked all the time of their own personal affairs. I realised that Messaoud's son intended to move into my house, and that didn't suit me at all. I went to Hubert's mother, Marie-Rose, and asked her to let me stay with her, while I waited for news from France. She agreed. I had a little bed taken over to her house, with some blankets, and I gave the nuns all the food that Papa had hoarded in those times of shortages. I stayed with Marie-Rose from 6 January to 6 February, when I left for France, accompanied by Mother Louis from Carthage. She was the person who opened the chest of drawers and gave me the retirement documents and the money she found there. A few days before he died, Papa had said to me, 'You see this money? Take care of it, that's put by for you, in case I'm not around to take care of you.'

I thought to myself, 'I shall die before you, and I shan't need all that,' as I had always been the most delicate one.

But man proposes and God disposes.

When the house had been closed up, I waited for news from Paris. It finally arrived.

Mother Louis from Carthage had written to my son René in Nice. He answered direct to my grandson Marcel in Algiers, asking him to put me up until he, René, could come himself and fetch me. Naturally I would have to meet the cost of his fares, but I had enough to cover these, out of the money Papa lad left in the drawer. I said goodbye for ever to this house which my husband had turned into a little jewel, and which the whole village envied.

I can still see Belkacem when the youngsters playing ball made dirty marks on the wall which he'd so carefully plastered and white-washed: he would take a sponge and a bucket of water and wash off the marks, while grumbling at the kids.

So I went with the nun to do my packing. I put everything tidily and methodically into the big trunk, but I made the mistake of not destroy-ing all the letters.*

I closed the doors, after giving everything to the nuns, even the old newspapers which, they said, would be useful to heat up their soup, and I left for Algiers with Mother Louis. We spent the night at the convent of El-Biar. The following Sunday, Charlotte came to fetch me. I think I stayed with her for two or three days before René arrived. I said goodbye to Mother Louis, after refunding her travel-ling expenses. At last René came to pick me up. Charlotte wouldn't accept any money in payment for my stay with her. We took the plane, flying via Corsica and we landed in Nice.

*

* Marguerite-Taos Amrouche adds a footnote to the effect that all the family correspondence, including letters from Jean Amrouche, was eventually returned to her by the nuns in Ighil-Ali.

At that time, I still had many illusions: I thought I would find a home after the one I had lost. I said to myself, 'I have lost my husband, my house, my country, but I still have my son.'

I was soon disillusioned. I'd given René the last of my money. For the first few days, René seemed pleased to have me with him, but his wife had not fully recovered from her recent confinement, and had sent for her grandmother, 'Mama Odette', to keep house for her, so there really wasn't any room . . .

After endless discussions, it was decided that I should leave Nice for Paris. Jean arrived to take charge of me. He said, 'Mother, my house is yours. You can share Pierre's room.'

So I left with Jean, but to begin with I preferred to go and stay with Marie-Louise-Taos; I stayed with her from March to June when Suzanne, Jean's wife, came to drive me to their house in Sargé-sur-Braye, where I spent the summer holidays with my daughter.

All this was nearly four years ago. Jean and Marie-Louise-Taos looked after my interests and took it in turns to give me a home and take care of me. I put myself entirely in their hands, as I had always lived under the guardianship and protection of my husband, who saw everything through my eyes.

I have lived through these years, going from one of my children to the other, but misfortune has knocked once again at my door: after more than four years, it was Jean's turn to go.

October 1958, Henri; January 1959, his father; April 1962, Jean. Since August 1939, five of my sons and their father: I have suffered six bereavements and I have survived all these misfortunes.

Sometimes I ask myself what kind of death I would choose so that I could fade away without pain, without watching myself die by degrees, like those who are paralysed.

Then I tell myself that I can still be of use to my daughter, and I try to console her a little. I would like to bequeath to her as many poems as possible, as many proverbs, and sayings . . . Oh! how beautiful the Kabyle language is, how poetic, how harmonious, when one knows it well . . . My countryfolk are so long-suffering in adversity, so obedient to the will of God, but this can only be fully understood if one can penetrate the language which was such a comfort to me during all my long periods of exile.

So I entreat my beloved daughter to have patience and to leave matters in God's hands, as Kabyle wisdom teaches us.

Her father used to say, 'Man strives, but God guides.'

For her I have tried to express, albeit clumsily, this guiding principle: 'Patience and courage! Everything runs its course and disappears from our sight, swept along in the river of eternity.'

Poems

Translator's Introduction

In the preceding pages Fadhma Aïth Mansour Amrouche tells us how, when her eldest son Paul enlisted in 1918 in the North African Light Cavalry at the outbreak of war – the first of her seven children to leave home – she turned to the songs and poems of her native country for solace: 'While I nursed my youngest child,' she writes, 'I nursed my sorrow and heavy tears ran down my face. How many songs have I sung since then! How many tears have I shed!'

Just over thirty years later, shattered by the deaths in quick succession of Paul, Louis and Noël, she again instinctively found a consolation for her grief in improvising songs and poems in her mother tongue, the Kabyle language. Before the war she had already started handing on to Jean and Marie-Louise-Taos her store of traditional Kabyle oral literature – tales, songs, poems, proverbs, legends, axioms – many of which they then had published in French. The songs that Marie-Louise learnt from her mother formed the repertoire for the recitals she gave in the original Kabyle throughout Europe and North Africa, many of which were recorded.

During the war, when Marie-Louise was living in Spain, her mother continued to send her more poems and songs as she remembered them. In 1940 Fadhma added her own original poems, written in Kabyle. Marie-Louise translated them into French and included them in her volume *Le grain magique*, a collection of Berber tales, proverbs and poems which ran into three editions. Five of these poems were composed in memory of Fadhma's dead sons: Paul-Mohand (Mohand, the Lion); Louis-Seghir (Seghir, the Tree-of-Sweetness); Noël-Saâdi (Saâdi, the Little-Bird). Two were intended to protect her daughter in her wartime exile in Spain.

I cannot claim that the following verses even approximate to the poetic quality of the originals. In attempting to render into English Taos Amrouche's French translations of her mother's improvisations in the Kabyle language, I am aware that I have no guide to their rhythmic patterns, musicality and intrinsic poetic qualities. I append them therefore, with this *caveat*, to Fadhma Amrouche's story of her life, for the added insight they give to her spiritual evolution and sensibilities.

Dorothy S. Blair

Be Not of Unquiet Spirit

Be not of unquiet spirit
For God is at hand.

As today our sorrow shall be lifted.
Winter will pass just as an ugly dream,
Cold days will leave us
And the clouds, the rain, the winds.
The grass will grow again
The meadows grow green again
And fill with unfolding flowers
And flocks will browse.

Summer will be restored to us
And the soil grow warm again
In the plains the corn will ripen
And the *fellahs* shall hunger no more.
The birds will sing still
In the trees, among the leaves.
The apricots and peaches,
Apples and mulberries,
The pears and figs
And all the abundant riches
Filling the world,
These are given by God to all his creatures.

But he said to them:
You shall labour.
He gave them death,
Old age and exile,
Sickness and tears
So that they might treasure all the good
And come before him with full hands,
After their sleep in the cold tomb.
What shall we take away of earthly goods?

These we shall leave to our heirs,
And we shall go with empty hands
From this ephemeral earth,
For naught is eternal save the face of God.

And God said to them:
If you sow righteousness
I shall receive you into my paradise.
Those who have hungered, then shall eat their fill,
Those who have suffered, then shall know my joy.
Those who were cold shall then be clad by me,
And those who wept shall laugh when at my side;
Those who were separated shall be united
In my paradise, the only infinite.

Be not of unquiet spirit,
Do not despair:
One day will see us before the face of God!

I am Like the Eagle

I am like the wounded eagle
The eagle shot between the wings.
All her children have flown away
And she weeps unceasingly.
Pity, O master of the winds,
Come to the aid of those who suffer.

I am like the mountain eagle,
On the highest rocky peak.
Nightly she gazes on the sky
Hoping to see, among the stars,
The faces of those who have flown away.

I pray to God and the friends of God
That they may appear to her in dreams –
Those children who have disappeared,
That she may see them in the life hereafter,
And then, maybe, know peace again.

Spirits of the West

Spirits of the West, be favourable
To my child, when in your midst,
Reach out a protecting hand to her.

Her hair is like a raven's wing
And blacker still her eyes and eyebrows,
Jet-black her long curled-back lashes.

Her flesh is like the full-blown roses
Fresh with the morning dew
Fallen during the night.

Her mouth with parted lips
Is a pomegranate,
And her teeth a necklace of pearls.

Her neck is such translucent amber,
So nearly transparent that when she drinks
One seems to see the water flowing

Her hands are tiny,
Like a child's,
With the softness of silk.

The Lord created her full of grace;
The days when her jewels enhance her beauty
May he preserve her from malevolent eyes.

Lord, protect her and fill her cup with joy.
Open wide all doors and clear every path for her.
People her solitude, make her exile light
And transfigure her in the eyes of all.

Would I Could Follow . . .

Would I could follow
To the land where souls take wing.
I would walk by night and day,
And across the heavens I would journey
To see once more the loved ones
Who have left me with wounded heart.

Who would care to go with me
To the land of the souls?'
We would go in search of them
And mingling with the birds
We would rise heavenwards
Towards my beloved children.

Would I could follow
To the land where souls take wing.
I would travel across the skies,
Trudging along in the wake of the stars,
To meet those loved ones
For whom my heart is plunged in mourning.

O Lord

O Lord, have pity on me
Thou who art unsurpassed
Thy will be done.

It shall be done, I know,
But deign to comfort me
Thou who hast given me all, and taken so much away.

Seghir, the pomegranate shoot,
Was so sweet of speech;
'Yes' was a flower on his lips.

Saâdi was a child,
Untroubled by care,
With singing mouth.

Mohand was the eagle
Sheltering with his wings
The children who had left me.

Oh! that day when they grew wings,
And, flinging themselves into the void,
They took flight and left me!

The Swallow

Swallow,
Take wing, fly speedily
To the land where my daughter is.

Settle to rest at her side,
Lean your head on her lap,
Take all her sorrows from her heart
And cast them down from the highest heavens
To the depth of the seas,
And leave her, in her exile,
With her heart rejoicing!

Behold me

Behold, I am gaunt, my face is clouded,
I am the yellowing leaf that loosens and falls.
My hair is white as a fleece,
My smile has withered round my sunken teeth,
My sight so dim
I can scarce make out a thorn.
The death of my beloved sons
Has left my heart bruised.

Behold, I stand here like a shadow,
My figure is bent,
I am the unknown soldier, struck down by a bullet.
Night and day, my tears flow
And there is no remedy for my immeasurable grief:
They fell all three within one year,
Never was I to see them again,
Sun, share my sorrow and hide your light too.

My heart cries out, my heart weeps
For the eyes of the eagle who is no more:
To this I shall never be resigned
He said to me, 'Mother, do not fear,
You can entrust my brothers to me,
I shall be a mother to each one of them,
And I shall open wide my home to them.'
I thought, 'No hurt can touch him,
He who shot up tall
Like an oak tree in the forest!'
But a storm blew up
And the mighty tree was suddenly uprooted
And laid low, in a far land.

My eyes know no respite from weeping.
Evening and morning I weep

For the children whose lives have ebbed:
Seghir, tree of sweetness
That bends in the breeze;
Saâdi, the little bird
That perched on the peach-tree branch
Singing from morning till night,
And Mohand the lion
Who bore away his brothers.

The storm came
And the thunder, lightning and wind,
The summer storm
Which uprooted my three sons
All three within one year.
Since then, I am inhabited by fear, one unending trembling:
If I have one friend, let him weep too!

Works by Jean Amrouche and Marguerite Taos

Jean Amrouche

Etoile secrète (Secret Star), poems.
Chantes berbères de Kabylie (Berber Songs from Kabylia), 1939.

Marie-Louise-Taos Amrouche

Under the name of Taos Amrouche

Le grain magique (The Magic Grain), Berber tales, poems, songs,
  proverbs from Kabylia, 1960.
Jacinthe noire (Black Hyacinth), a novel, 1947, re-ed. 1972.

Under the name of Marguerite Taos

Rue des Tambourins, autobiographical novel, 1960.

Records and cassettes

Florilège de chants berbères de Kabylie (Berber Songs from
  Kabylia).
Chants de processions, Méditations et danses sacrées berbères
  (Berber processional songs, meditations and sacred dances).
Chants de l'Atlas. Tradition millénaire des Berbères d'Algérie
  (Songs from the Atlas, a thousand-year-old tradition from the
  Berbers of Algeria).

Letter from Jean Amrouche to his Mother

Paris, 16 April 1945

Dear Mother,

I have been meaning to write you a long letter for several weeks. As I walk through the streets of Paris I sometimes imagine that you are holding my arm. We are walking very very slowly, as we used to when we took our evening stroll beside the railway line in Radès. You drag your poor feet along in your old sandals; you cross your faded shawl over your chest. But the eyes that you dart all around you are those of a mischievous girl, missing nothing of the muted colours of the sky or of the stars that beckon us. An immeasurable peace rises up with the fragrance from the gardens and mingles with the peace that descends from the sky.

And I think sadly that life will not grant us many more occasions to take these strolls before the house closes its wings over us for the night. I never recall our house in Radès without being moved to tears. It is so heavy with memories, so full of dreams in which images of despair mingle with those illuminated with joy – rarer, alas! than the former – to compose a bitter-sweet harmony which is like the very music of its soul.

Little mother, sweet mother, patient, resigned mother, always so full of courage in your sorrows! Do you have any inkling that your little Jeannot still clings to your skirts? that he will never be cured of his childhood, and that, wherever he goes, whatever he does, you are with him? Not as a fugitive image that flashes through his memory, but in the air he breathes and without which he would suffocate?

How are you keeping, this springtide, which is more like summer? How do you manage with all the housework? In the long run, all the burdens fall on you and father. After more than fifty years of drudgery you have the right to rest, and none of your children has yet been in a position to ensure this for you.

But, little mother, you are our secret miracle. For, in spite of the toil which wears out body and soul, God has granted you the rarest grace: beneath your wrinkles and white hair, you have retained a youthful heart and a fount of joy which gushes forth from your tired eyes, like a spring hidden beneath the rocks.

If Marie-Louise and I both have some feeling for poetry and art, we owe it all to you. You have given us everything, you have handed on to us the message from our native soil and from our dead. But your task is not yet finished, little mother. Now, when I am just beginning to see the direction that my main work should take, I appeal to you once more. You must write down every single thing that you can remember about your life, not just as the mood takes you, or according to the inspiration of the moment, but everything. It will require an enormous effort. But just keep in mind, little mother, that you must not let your childhood and all that you experienced in Kabylia be lost. A priceless lesson can be learnt from this. And for me it will be a sacred trust. I beg you, little mother, think seriously about my request . . .

Your most affectionate son,
Jeannot
(Jean Amrouche)

Note from Fadhma Amrouche to her Son

Maxula-Radès, 1 August 1946

To my son Jean,

I bequeath you this story, which is the account of my life, for you to do what you like with, after my death.

This story is true, not one episode has been invented, all that happened before my birth was told me by my mother as soon as I was old enough to understand. I have written this story, because I think it deserves to be known to all of you.

If you ever decide to do anything with this, I would like all the proper names to be suppressed, and if you make it into a novel, then all the profits should be shared among your brothers and sister, when you have deducted your own expenses and taken your own work into account. Once this story is completed, it will be sealed and entrusted to your father who will hand it to you after my death.

I wrote this story in memory of my beloved mother and of Mme Malaval who gave me my spiritual life.

1 August   31 August 1946
M. Amrouche

If I should not be able to have this manuscript published in my lifetime, I entrust to my daughter Marguerite Taos Amrouch, and to her alone, the exclusive responsibility to see that it is published without any modifications, or with only minor changes relating to the style.

Paris, 13 December 1964
Marguerite Fadhma Aïth Mansour Amrouche

Glossary

araba	a light cart, usually two-wheeled, drawn by a mule or donkey
burnouse	a voluminous woollen cloak with a hood, worn chiefly by men in North Africa
chekchouka	a vegetable dish with one or more eggs cooked on top or mixed with the vegetables (rather like a Spanish omelette)
couscous	a dish made of granulated flour, usually semolina, which the women pound or 'roll' before steaming over a meat and/or vegetable broth
douar	a small village or settlement
fellah	a peasant, farm labourer
filali	a type of embroidery, originating in Morocco
fouta	a sarong-like garment, worn tied around the waist
galette	a flat cake or type of pancake made from flour (wheat, buckwheat or cornflour, as available), eggs and butter or oil, cooked under the ashes or on top of a stove
gandoura	a loose, sleeveless tunic
gourbi	a small shack
gennour	an imposing turban, worn by the men of the Aïth-Abbas region of La Petite Kabylie
kabkabs	stilts for walking in deep snow
kadi (*cadi* or *kaïd*)	Muslim judge, fulfilling civil as well as religious functions
kanoun	a brazier
khammès	a person who works land rented from a landowner, to whom he gives a share of the crop

khelkhal   an ankle bracelet

khoufi   a basket for measuring out grain

Llala (or *Lla*)   a title of respect used to address an older woman

marabout   a Muslim holy man or leader, whose advice is sought on secular as well as religious matters

Roumi   a pejorative term applied to foreigners and, by extension, to converted Algerians

seroual   loose, baggy trousers

spahi   a member of the Algerian cavalry in the service of the French

tajmaât   the village assembly place